Early Childhood
Literature Sharing Programs
in Libraries

Early Childhood Literature Sharing Programs in Libraries

Ann D. Carlson

LIBRARY PROFESSIONAL PUBLICATIONS
1985

First published in 1985 as a
Library Professional Publication,
an imprint of The Shoe String Press, Inc.,
Hamden, Connecticut 06514

Printed in the United States of America

Library of Congress Cataloging-in-Publication Data
Carlson, Ann D., 1952-
Early childhood literature sharing programs in libraries.

Based on the author's thesis ▶
(doctoral—Columbia University, 1983).
Bibliography: p.
Includes index.
1. Libraries, Children's—Activity programs.
2. Storytelling. 3. Children—Books and reading.
4. Reading (Preschool) I. Title.
Z718.3.C37   1985   027.62′5   85-13028
ISBN 0-208-02068-3
ISBN 0-208-02074-8 (pbk.)

To
Kay Vandergrift,
Jane Hannigan,
and
Carolyn Peterson

Contents

Acknowledgments

This book is based on my dissertation written in the School of Library Service at Columbia University. I would like to express my gratitude to Kay Vandergrift, my advisor, and Leslie Williams, of Teachers College, my second reader.

I also wish to thank Harriet Cuffaro of Bank Street College of Education, Irene Shagaki of New York University, Patricia Vardin of Teachers College, Daniel Stern of the Payne Whitney Clinic, and Jeanna Gollobin of the Soho Center for Arts and Education for their time and valuable suggestions regarding the schema.

I am indebted to the librarians who participated in the study and to Children's Services Consultants at various state libraries who helped me locate the participants. Without their help there would have been no study.

Thanks are also due to Mary Carlson who designed the cover illustration of my questionnaire, and to Ates Dagli who read the manuscript and made helpful criticisms.

Introduction

During the past two decades, the importance of a child's first few years has come to be more fully recognized in the field of child development. Research dealing with the capabilities of infants and young children, their language development, and early environmental interactions and stimulation has provided a great amount of early childhood development information. Much of this information presents a direct challenge to parents because this research has also shown the importance of the parents' role in influencing the development of their young children.

These research findings have provided some librarians with the impetus for developing programs designed for a new clientele. Since the early 1970s, a growing number of public libraries across the country have initiated early childhood literature sharing programs, that is, storytimes for children under three years of age and informational programs for parents and caregivers of such children. The success of the programs they modeled and reported in the library press spurred others to follow suit.

With the proliferation of these early childhood literature sharing programs in libraries, a need existed to determine if librarians who offered programs in this area were aware of the recent early childhood development information and its implications for literature sharing programs. Of interest also was whether their awareness was correlated with their institutional and personal characteristics and attitudes.

I decided to make these questions the subject of the research undertaken in partial fulfillment of requirements for the doctorate in library science at Columbia University from 1981 to 1983. It first occurred to me to do this in June 1980 during an American Library Association conference in New York City when I heard a children's librarian say that she could not understand why everyone was making such a big deal about toddler storytimes since, "after all, a two-year-old is just a short three-year-old."

The purpose of the study was two-fold. The first purpose was to develop a schema that would link analysis of the information about child development from birth to three years of age with literature sharing implications for library programs. The schema would be reviewed for accuracy by early childhood specialists. The second purpose was to determine if the practices and attitudes of librarians corresponded to this schema, and if those practices and attitudes are independent of certain institutional and personal characteristics. Data for accomplishing this second purpose was gathered by asking librarians in the United States who offer early childhood literature sharing programs to complete a mail survey questionnaire. Seventy-eight percent, or 253 of the 324 librarians thought to have such programs provided responses suitable for analysis.

The schema is the heart of this book. Based solidly upon research, it turned out to coincide also with the instinctive behaviors of the children's librarians who were matching library activities to what they knew about very young children before there was much proof that they were doing the right things. I hope that it will encourage and help many more children's librarians across the country to offer early childhood literature sharing programs—word, rhyme and rhythm experiences for children under the age of three, plus informational programs for parents, and other caregivers. It is these adults who will have the sustained, ongoing opportunity to make the most of these irretrievable-if-lost 36 months for mental growth and learning—to love books, among many other things. This outline of the growth patterns and potentials of 0-6 month-olds, 7-14 month-olds, 15-24 month-olds and 25-36 month-olds matched with related literature and library activities can make librarians feel confident that the programs are eminently worthwhile and that they are taking full advantage of growth patterns that influence development.

1

Development of Library Programs for Children under Three Years of Age and for Parents and Caregivers

"Daily it grows more apparent that the program of the [library with services for parents and their young children] is irrevocably tied up with a broad program of systematic study of the infant and young child's nature and needs and his wider family relationship." One may think that this statement was made recently, but it was not. It was in fact written nearly fifty years ago by a librarian who realized, along with other librarians, that "serious consideration should be given to this vitally important matter of how and when to instill the love of books and reading in the child."[1]

It is said that nearly every so-called innovation has its historical roots, and this is indeed the case for library programs for parents and their very young children.

Services and Programs in the 1930s

Historically, some children's librarians have recognized the need for providing services to parents and their young children. As early as 1929, the ALA Committee on Cooperation with the National Congress of Parents and Teachers published *The Parents' Bookshelf*,[2] an annotated list of books and pamphlets which was "compiled with the needs of the child in mind." This bibliography included materials discussing the importance of play (for example, *Play Life in the First Eight Years* [1916] and *Permanent Play Materials for Young Children* [1926]), psychological development (*A Practical Psychology of Babyhood*

[1925]), and physical development (*Health of the Runabout Child* [1924] and *From Infancy to Childhood* [1925]).[3]

During the mid-1930s, the library literature reported more than a dozen public libraries that had established special parent rooms or alcoves within children's rooms or departments.[4] Many of these special areas were called Mothers' Rooms, and the popularity of these rooms is reflected by the fact that the 1936-1939 *Library Literature* listed the new subject heading "Mothers' Rooms."[5]

The most notable and well documented of these was the Mothers' Room established in 1935 in the children's department of the Youngstown (Ohio) Public Library, which was directed by Clarence Sumner. There are seven citations referring to this in the 1936-1939 *Library Literature* alone. In 1936, John Creager claimed that "the book and periodical collection serve a dual purpose. For the parent who wants something on child training problems there is a wealth of books and current magazines . . . ; then there is a large collection of picture and story books for the child of six weeks, or six years. The library gives the mothers a list of books of several types, and sheets containing actual finger plays, riding songs, and lullabies . . . . These are essential for Baby's development."[6]

In a book written in 1936 called *The Birthright of Babyhood,* Sumner explained the reason for the Mothers' Room in his library:

> Thus it was we visioned . . . a room with a program whereby the mother could be helped to build up a background of good reading for her little child. For many years the Children's Room has been an established department of every public library. . . . Then why not a Mothers' Room designed for the mother and child to help build a background of good books from babyhood? The Mothers' Room would thus serve as the "builder" and "feeder" for the Children's Room, being the logical first unit in the program of the public library.[7]

A feature of the Youngstown Public Library's Mothers' Room was an annual "Mothers' Institute." The first of these, held in March 1936, had the slogan "Begin in Babyhood." The leader of the first Institute was Dr. Garry C. Myers, head of the Department of Parent Education at Western Reserve University, who spoke to 225 mothers on subjects such as "Developing the Young Child" and "Letting the Little Child Learn at Home." Evening sessions for nursery school teachers were also included in the Institute when Dr. Myers spoke on "The Educational Implications of the Mothers' Room."[8]

The Second Mothers' Institute was held in November 1937 when "about a thousand people attended the five sessions." The scope of publicity for this event is interesting to note: "A personal message was sent to the mother of each child born in Mahoning County, Ohio, in the four years preceding the Institute. This included more than twelve thousand mothers."[9] A 1936 *Library Journal* article described the library service and program:

> The project of a Mothers' Room and a Mothers' Institute in a public library . . . has been planned as a joint adult and pre-school educational program. Mothers of very young infants are urged to start immediately, a few months after the child is born, with the material and program offered by the Mothers' Room. The object is not to teach the small child to read before it enters school. . . . But parents should begin early to read stories and poems to their young children, to impress upon their minds the pleasures that may be derived from books.[10]

In 1938 the Youngstown Public Library initiated another phase in the work of the Mothers' Room by employing a lecturer and consultant who presented "two lectures every other week" in the area of children's reading, the importance of family relationships, and the psychological and physical training of the child.[11]

The rationale for the Mothers' Room is succinctly described by Martha Goodman:

The reading of stories to small children in the home is emphasized in its relation to the companionship and intimate comradeship that thereby develop between child and parent. It helps to develop a happy family atmosphere. . . . The child's imagination and vocabulary are developed rapidly by this plan long before it enters school. This is not forcing the child, simply carrying him along and greatly aiding his mental development. Educators and librarians everywhere are concerned that children, youth and adults keep on reading good books. Whether or not they grow up to be readers will depend largely upon the influence brought to bear upon them in their early years. If they have been given the best in infancy and childhood they will learn to discriminate as to what has charm and beauty in content and language as they grow older.[12]

Garry Myers and Clarence Sumner continued to state their case for Mothers' Rooms, "the dual program of service to parents and to children alike," in their book, *Books and Babies*.[13] The chapters of this delightful book address topics such as "Intelligent Parenthood," "Books and Happy Guidance of the Young Child," "Imaginative Stories and Mental Health," and "Reading Rather than Telling Stories."

In *Books and Babies,* Myers and Sumner make statements that twenty-five years later would be topics of much detailed research in the field of child psychology:

A very important part of the child's training has been completed by the time he enters school. His education has been going on from the moment of his birth. It is in these early years that many permanent patterns of attitudes and habits have been forming. The little child not only is very impressionable, acquiring basic attitudes and habits, but his parents, being more impressionable than they will be later, are also inclined to acquire certain attitudes and habits toward the child which tend to persist. Indeed, the parents' early attitude in respect to parenthood may be just as significant as the early attitudes which the child acquires.[14]

Services and Programs in the
1940s through the 1960s

In the introduction of Sumner's book, *The Birthright of Babyhood,* Garry Myers states that "this new enterprise of Sumner's is destined, no doubt, soon to be nation-wide and eventually world-wide. . . . It focuses in a very dramatic way many of the finest parent-child experiences of the age and is buttressed by good sound principles of modern psychology."[15] However, this expectation did not become a reality during Sumner's lifetime. Little mention of Mothers' Rooms in the Youngstown Public Library or elsewhere in this country is found after 1942. In fact, *Library Literature* deleted the subject heading after this date.

One could speculate that the decline of the programs and services of Mothers' Rooms could be attributed to the advent of World War II. The author of a 1943 article, "Storytelling: A Wartime Activity," claims that during that time mothers were "devoting all or part of their time to war activities," and, therefore, had less time to visit Mothers' Rooms.[16] Even though parent education programs in some libraries continued to exist for a while, it appears that for the most part these programs were not specifically designed for parents of children under three years of age.[17]

During the decades of the 1940s through the 1960s, children's librarians turned their attention to a new type of preschool programming, the preschool story hour. The history of the preschool story hour is well documented, and eventually these programs came to be a part of basic library service.[18]

From the beginning, preschool story hours by and large have been restricted to children over three years of age (as exemplified in the title of a 1950's article, "Just under Three Is a Little too Young"),[19] and parent education has not been a part of their purpose. In a 1947 article, one librarian claims: "There are, of course, many arguments favoring the theory that the parent profits by attending the story hour. I do not deny that this may be true in some cases, but in general we do not hold our story hours for the training of parents."[20] Parents traditionally have not participated in these programs, thereby making them librarian-child-oriented rather than like the parent-child-oriented services of the Mothers' Rooms.

Services and Programs in the 1970s

During the 1970's, however, there was a resurgence of library programs and services for children under three years of age and for their parents, along with a variety of services and programs for child care personnel and other adults who work with young children. This is reflected by the fact that in 1974, *Library Literature* included two new subject headings under "Public Libraries,"—services to parents, and, services to preschoolers.

The Children's Services Division of the ALA also recognized this growing trend, and in 1972 an ad hoc Preschool Services and Parent Education Committee was established and soon became an official committee.[21] This was followed by the appearance of articles, books, and films which expressed the need to provide programs and services to parents (and other adults) and their children under three years of age. Some examples are: Sandra Sivulich's "Ideas Exchange: Public Libraries and Early Childhood Education," which appeared in a 1977 library publication whose next issue included Diana Young's, "Parents, Children, Libraries," and Faith Hektoen's "Parents Support Programs;" the book *Start Early for an Early Start* edited by Ferne Johnson; and Orlando Public Library's film, *What's so Great about Books?*[22]

The variety of both in-house and outreach programs and services for parents, caregivers and children under age three is extensive. Public libraries initiated information and referral services for parents and caregivers of young children, such as the one described by Linda Blaha in "An Information and Referral Service for Parents of Preschool Children."[23] Programs and services for child care centers, such as those described by Carolyn Peterson in "Sharing Literature with Children," Jean Rustici in "Public Library and Child Care Center Relationship," and Penny Wilson and Peggy Abramo in "Early Childhood Programs for Adults—Public Library Reaches Out" also were reported in library publications.[24] Faith Hektoen, Martha Barnes, and Nancy DeSalvo described various informational programs for parents of young children.[25]

Libraries were also providing books for parents in the children's rooms—a service that was a very popular feature of the 1930s Mothers' Rooms. During the 1970s, librarians described special parenting and child development book collections in children's departments, such as Grace Ruth's "Parenting Collection."[26] New York Public Library's parenting and child development collection at the Early Childhood Resource and Information Center was a model collection of materials for teachers, parents, and other adults who interact with young children.[27]

Articles about toy lending services for young children in public libraries also appeared in the literature. In 1974, *Library Journal* reported such services, and other articles pointed out the benefits of toys.[28]

Grant funding for large scale preschool programs in libraries enabled a few children's departments to create a variety of programs and services to parents, caregivers, and young children. Two of the best reported were the Pre-School Experience Program at the Public Library of Columbus and Franklin County, Ohio, and Project Little Kids at the Greenville (South Carolina) Public Library.[29]

Around the mid-70s, reports of a new type of library service began to appear in the literature by libraries that did not receive grant funding: the storytime for children under three years of age. Juliet Markowsky's "Storytime for Toddlers" was one of the first lengthy articles about toddler storytime programming in a public library. Other articles, such as Nancy DeSalvo's "The Terrific Two's," Martha Barnes's "Library Service to Very Young Children and Their Parents in Westchester County," Nancy Kewish's "South Euclid's Pilot Project for Two-Year-Olds and Parents," and Bonnie Fowler's "Toddlers' Storytimes," also described toddler programs in various libraries across the country.[30]

Along with toddler storytimes, librarians initiated programs for still younger children—infants. These programs for the most part centered on parent education, such as the "Catch 'em in the Cradle" service at Orlando Public Library, and San Francisco Public Library's "You, Your New Baby and the Library."[31]

It is apparent that the traditional reference to the three-to-six year old child had, by the end of the 1970s, been expanded so that, as Amy Kellman says, "from birth on the child has a place in the library's scheme of things."[32] Librarians across the country were initiating a spectrum of programs for children under three years of age and their parents and/or caregivers. Literature sharing programs center around children's literature geared to young children and appropriate literature-related activities, such as finger plays, songs, simple poems and nursery rhymes, flannel board stories, etc. The main purpose of these programs is to encourage interest in books in young children.

2

Overview of Recent Changes in the Study of Early Childhood Development

The first three years of a child's life is undeniably a period of rapid growth. It is during this period that most children learn to walk, talk, manipulate objects, and feed and toilet themselves. They develop socially, emotionally, and intellectually as they interact with their environments and deal with objects and people in those environments.

The study of children has a long history. Dietrich Tiedemann's *Beobachtungen über die Entwickelung der Seelenfähigkeiten bei Kindern,*[1] first published in 1787, is usually regarded as the first attempt to make a series of scientific observations on the behavior of young children. Chronicling the development of a child born over 200 years ago, his words opened the door for the modern study of young children: "experience and practice teach us to use our senses and perceive correctly . . . [and] the mental faculties develop slowly [and] successively."[2]

However, it has been during the past two decades that child development specialists have come to realize the importance of a child's first few years. As Jerome Kagan states in *The Growth of the Child: Reflections on Human Development:* "Twenty years ago the study of infancy was a wasteland. Today we have a little more understanding [of infancy] and have come to regard that period as more dynamic and more transient."[3]

The major work which has occurred since the 1960s includes and relates to: increased research emphasis on cognition, especially the work of Piaget;[4] effects of early environmental stimulation on later cognitive functioning and the related issue of compensatory education; systematic investigation of the capabilities of infants; the development of both syntactic and semantic aspects of language; more thorough and methodologically sounder research on parent-child relations as antecedents of later personality development; [and] increased concern with social behavior.[5]

Changes in the Field: *Carmichael's Manual*

A good indicator of the changes in the field of child development can be seen by examining the various editions of the *Manual of Child Psychology*,[6] or as it is commonly referred to, *Carmichael's Manual*. This sourcebook on child psychology and development has had three editions to date—in 1946, 1954, and 1970. Each *Manual* is comprised of chapters on various aspects of child development written by experts, and the purpose of these chapters is to provide an accurate picture of the current state of knowledge, thereby reflecting a comprehensive view of the thinking and the research of the time.

While a comparison of the editions shows a basic objective in all of them to be a description of the roots of child behavior, and an expression of the need for further research, the 1970 edition (which is a two-volume *Manual*) reveals a marked increase in the amount of research and publications devoted to child psychology. For example, Pratt's chapter, "The Neonate," in the 1946 and 1954 editions has a bibliography that includes about 500 studies concerning the young child, while Kessen, Haith, and Salapatek's chapter, "Human Infancy," in the 1970 edition has a bibliography that cites over 2,000 studies.[7]

Moreover, the later edition differs by something more important than simply recording the prodigious number of studies in the field; it reflects the theoretical emphasis placed on the importance of *explaining* child behavior, not just describing it. For example, Pratt's chapter in the early editions centers on descriptions of the young child, detailing physical characteristics such as heartbeat, metabolism, digestion ("The stomach empties in 4 to 5 hours at most; the small intestines in 7 to 8 hours . . . "), secretion, and so forth. Pratt's discussion reflects the fact that many studies of the time were in fact physiological in nature. In contrast, the 1970 edition reveals that the later researchers sought more facts about the changes in young children's abilities and behavior that relate to development, and more importantly, an understanding of how these changes occur.

This drive for explanations consequently stimulated an interest in more theory-building, and it is reflected in the various *Manual* editions. The early editions contain only one theoretical chapter, "Behavior and Development as a Function of Total Situation,"[8] focusing on the Lewinian theory which has not had a lasting impact on the field. In contrast, the 1970 edition contains numerous chapters devoted entirely to theory (there are ten chapters on cognitive development theory alone) in addition to theoretical issues being addressed in nearly all lengthy chapters. It is clear that theory-building has played an important role in the direction of empirical research, especially in the area of cognitive development where Piaget's theories have engendered hypotheses for research.

A comparison of the editions of the *Manual* indicates the following changes in child psychology: (1) the "knowledge explosion" of relevant literature, (2) the increase in sophistication and degree of specialization, and (3) the change in emphasis of child psychology from *what* young children perceive to *how* young children gather information from the world around them and *how* they react to what they perceive.

Changes in the Field: Information for Parents

While the research in *Carmichael's Manual* is very scholarly, much current research that recognizes the importance of a child's first few years has become available in a more popular form in a number of books. One such book is the best-selling *The First Three Years of Life* by Burton White. In the preface White claims: "My own studies, as well as the work of many others, have clearly indicated that the experiences of those first years are far more important than we had previously thought. In their everyday activities, infants and toddlers form the foundations of *all* later development."[9] Ten years earlier, Benjamin Bloom argued in *Stability and Change in Human Character* that the intellectual skills of the adult can be presaged in the first five years of life.[10]

In addition to White's book, an outpouring of non-technical books for parents by such highly regarded authorities as Arnold Gesell, Frances Ilg and Louise Ames, T. Berry Brazelton, and Ira Gordon appeared.[11]

Along with the importance of a child's first few years, recognition of the parents' role in influencing the development of their young children has also surfaced in the research of the past two decades. This recognition, for example, led to the directives for inclusion of parents in all functioning phases of one of the federal government's War on Poverty programs, Project Head Start.[12] Retrospective analysis of research connected with Head Start and other programs has led to a growing awareness of the importance of parental involvement in producing healthy, happy, and active child-learners, regardless of whether the child is in formal child care or in the care of parents or caregivers.[13]

After an in-depth review of the effects of a variety of early childhood programs, some of which included parent participation and some of which did not, Urie Bronfenbrenner concludes: "The evidence indicates that the family is the most effective and economical system for fostering and sustaining the development of the child. . . . The involvement of the parents as partners in the enterprise provides an on-going system which can reinforce the effects of the program while it is in operation, and help sustain them after the program ends."[14]

As a result of the belief that parents should be active in their children's development, a variety of programs and information outlets have been and are continuing to be developed. All around us we see increasing numbers of books, magazines, pamphlets, newspaper columns, training classes, parent/child play groups, and parent discussion groups designed to help parents. These programs and information outlets focus on parent growth as well as on the growth of the young child. Since parents are a child's most important adults and earliest and most continuous teachers, more and more attention has been given not only to the importance of child development and its implications, but also to the importance and development of parental attitudes and competencies.

3

Developing the Rationale for Introducing Young Children to Literature

With the abundance of studies on child development, many parents and educators have become increasingly aware of the importance of introducing literature and literature-related activities to young children. Dorothy Butler claims: "It is my belief that there is no 'parents' aid which can compare with the book in its capacity to establish and maintain a relationship with a child. Its effects extend far beyond the covers of the actual book, and invade every aspect of life."[1] Another educator, Linda Lamme, makes a similar claim when she says: "Ours is a print-oriented society; books of many types are abundantly available. Hence, it is a natural part of our child-rearing practices to introduce the young child to books very early. We introduce them for pleasure, not instruction."[2]

Several authors have expressed the importance of introducing the riches of literature and the literature-related activities to young children. Aidan Chambers described it best when he said: "We have to acknowledge that the best and most lasting success comes only when the home environment is right-minded. . . . We have, in fact, at last begun to recognize that any child who comes to school at five without certain kinds of literary experiences is a deprived child in whose growth there are deficiencies already too difficult to make good."[3]

A number of books have recently appeared that are designed to offer parents a variety of ideas for getting young children involved with literature and literature-related activities. For example, there are Dorothy Butler's *Babies Need Books;* Susan M. Glazer's *Getting*

Ready to Read: Creating Readers from Birth through Six; and Linda Lamme's *Raising Readers: A Guide to Sharing Literature with Young Children.*[4]

These books share a common belief about the value of exposing literature to young children; however, this is not an entirely new revelation. For generations parents have recited Mother Goose nursery rhymes, sung songs, told simple stories and participated in finger plays with their young children. There were also a number of books, such as Annis Duff's *Bequest of Wings* (1944), May Lamberton Becker's *First Adventures in Reading* (1936), Dorothy White's *Books before Five* (1954), and Nancy Larrick's *A Parent's Guide to Children's Reading* (1958) that encouraged parents to share literature with their young children.[5] However, with the recent findings about the capacities of young children, writers today have research as well as instinct and experience on which to base their beliefs.

The rationale for library programs for young children and parents is based on the research findings pertaining to young children's learning along with the products of research about parent education. In 1979, Linda Lamme provided an educator's rationale for library programs for young children. Her rationale included the following four points which are supported by research in the field.[6]

(1) A child's receptive language begins at birth, and parents have a great impact upon their child's language development if they talk, sing, and read to their young children. Book language is generally more complex than spoken language; therefore, reading to a young child exposes the child to more sophisticated language than is generally heard in family conversation.

A great amount of research has been conducted during the past fifteen years on the subject of language acquisition. As J.H. Flavell states: "A truly extraordinary amount of language development gets accomplished during the early childhood period—in fact, we have only recently begun to appreciate just *how* much."[7]

(2) Library programs for young children and parents establish routines and form habits. If parents can be encouraged to make singing, talking and reading a part of their daily schedules, and if they regularly visit the library, they not only set up routine behavior for their young children, but also begin to develop expectations, behavior patterns, and lifetime reading habits for the future.

(3) Library programs establish reading readiness. Young children need repeated exposure to printed language, which, in turn, will develop the child's linguistic awareness. Understandings that young children who are read to will acquire include: the fact that pictures have meaning; that pictures are different from words; that pages turn from right to left; that books have a front and a back, and a right side up; and that stories have a structure.

In addition, young children exposed repeatedly to literature develop a "sense of story." The child will in time develop an overall concept of what a story is, a framework to which readiness skills can later be attached. Skills taught in isolation, away from the real world of books to which they belong, are far more difficult for children to learn, and far less meaningful because they are often memorized in isolation.

In 1978, William Teal published the results of a study he had conducted about early readers. From his review of a large number of investigations of children who read at an early age, Teal deduced four factors which were associated with the backgrounds of the readers: (1) there was an availability and range of printed materials in the child's environment, (2) reading was "done" in an environment created by parents reading to the child and by parents acting as models for reading behavior, (3) the environment facilitated contact with paper and pencil, and (4) parents and other significant people in the child's life responded to the child's attempt to make sense of the printed word in "reading activities."[8]

(4) Library programs for young children and parents provide enjoyment. In addition to enjoying library programs, young children and parents will learn that reading together is a pleasurable activity. Birth to three years of age is the ideal time to learn to value books and reading.

Developing the Schema

As previously mentioned, one of the purposes of this study was to review and analyze the current knowledge of child development from birth to three years of age and to derive its implications for what librarians should be doing in their programs. For lack of a better term, this was called a "schema," which in the broad sense is defined as an outline. The schema then served as the basis for the queries made in the survey questionnaire that was sent to librarians who offer early childhood programs.

Sources

In order to develop the schema, several kinds of resource books were reviewed. General child development texts, such as Stone and Church's *Childhood and Adolescence* served as a starting point for the analysis.[9] Eleanor Willemsen's *Understanding Infancy* provided a detailed review of the development of young children drawn from the research literature since the mid-1960s.[10]

The study of child development is more, of course, than simply a search for a collection of facts. Therefore, information from various theoretical orientations, or schools of thought, was analyzed. The cognitive theory of Jean Piaget played a very important role in the development of the schema. Since Piaget's theories so clearly and specifically define the intellectual development in young children, heavy emphasis was placed on the theories provided by him and his empirical followers. Four of Piaget's works were included in the analysis: *The Psychology of the Child,* which is an excellent summary of his theories; *Construction of Reality in the Child* and *The Origins of Intelligence in the Child* which describe the sensori-motor period of development (from birth to two years of age); and, *Play, Dreams and Imitation in Childhood* which describes the preconceptual period of development (from two to four years of age).[11]

The affective, or psychoanalytic, theory of Erik Erikson also played a role in the development of the schema, although to a lesser extent than did Piaget's theory. Erikson's theory about the emotional development of young children, especially his concept of phases of acquiring a sense of basic trust and of acquiring a sense of autonomy, presented in his *Childhood and Society,* was analyzed.[12] The behavioral theory of Robert Sears also influenced the schema, but to a much lesser extent. Analysis was made also of Sears's research and essays on learning theories, which explore some aspects of child rearing and describe the impact of environmental forces on child development.[13]

Even though the three theoretical approaches represented by the theories of Piaget, Erikson, and Sears have marked differences in terms of procedures and perspectives, their findings are by no means entirely contradictory; in fact, at times they seem to be strikingly parallel. They deal, for the most part, with different aspects or planes of child development; however, all three agree that complexity in functioning increases as the child becomes older.

As previously stated, great emphasis was placed on Piaget's theories in the development of the schema. Therefore, sources which interpret and offer evidence about these theories were also analyzed. Two of the most heavily used were J. McVicker Hunt's classic, *Intelligence and Experience,* which describes the development of intelligence and the testing of Piaget's theories, and the Uzgiris-Hunt scales in *Assessment in Infancy,* since the evidence from Ina Uzgiris about these scales strongly supports Piaget's theories of development.[14]

Another source was T.G.R. Bower. Two of his works, *A Primer of Infant Development* and *Development in Infancy,* describe his research dealing with the capabilities of infants.[15] Bower's major contribution to the field is showing that infants' perceptions must be separated from their motor abilities. It is considered that Bower's view does not conflict with Piaget's but rather extends and clarifies it.

Prelanguage development and language development information sources were analyzed. Sections of previously mentioned sources—Piaget, Bower, Uzgiris and Hunt, and the general textbooks—address this topic, just as sections in many of the sources which follow do. One specialized text, Dale's *Language Development,* was used.[16]

Other specialized texts, especially those from university-based centers, were consulted for the purposes of this schema. The work of Arnold Gesell and his associates at Yale has played an important role in child development. *Infant and Child in the Culture of Today,* along with *The Gesell Institute's Child from One to Six* provided maturational information.[17] Also included was information from Burton White's *Human Infants: Experience and Psychological Development* (which is also presented in White and Watts's *Experience and Environment.*[18] His suggestions for optimizing development during a child's early years were based on his research at Harvard, and they were analyzed for the development of this schema.

In addition to these somewhat technical sources, a number of popularized books on child development,

intended mainly for parents, were consulted. Burton
White's *The First Three Years of Life* was a useful
resource. Information from Mary Ann Pulaski's *Your
Baby's Mind and How It Grows: Piaget's Theory
for Parents,* along with Carol Tomlinson-Keasey's
Child's Eye View—both interesting and informative
books—were also analyzed.[19] The list of sources mentioned is by no means exhaustive, but it is representa-
tive of the types of works consulted for the development
of the schema.

Framework of the Schema

With the large amount of early childhood development
information gleaned from the sources used, a suitable
and manageable framework for organizing the information was needed. Various frameworks were considered, such as organizing according to different classes
of behavior, e.g., motor, sensory, social, language, etc.;
according to the children's needs, such as the framework Bettye Caldwell used to organize her "Conceptual
Schema for Planning and Implementing an Infant
Care Program";[20] or according to a structured assessment scale similar to a mental and motor scale.

After due consideration, the early childhood development information was outlined with predominant
developmental characteristics of children from birth to
three years of age arranged according to four growth
periods—0 to 6 months, 7 to 14 months, 15 to 24 months,
and 25 to 36 months. The breakdown of growth into
these four periods, for the most part, corresponds to
typical growth spurts in young children. The birth to 6
months of age growth period is a prelocomotive time for
infants when, even though they have an enormous
impact on their environment, experiences in the
environment are brought to them. The 7 to 14 months of
age growth period is one characterized by a locomobil-
ity which enables toddlers (or soon to be toddlers) to
explore their environment actively for the first time. It

is also a period of language use (speech, usually in the form of sounds). The 15 to 24 months growth period is a time of increasing social development, new motor skills, and expressive language for toddlers. By the 25 to 36 months growth period, the two-to-three-year-olds are utilizing increased mental powers, essaying complex language with conversational sequences, and displaying growing autonomy.

Since a developmental continuum for children exists, and children move along it at different rates, any organizational framework—whether it is classes of behavior, children's needs, or growth periods—will appear arbitrary. Even though it is arranged according to growth periods, this framework should not imply that all children will conform to these landmarks. The individual child develops according to his or her own timing; and within a particular growth pattern, the child may move at varied rates—sometimes rapidly and at other times slowly.

This schema, therefore, describes developmental growth for children *in general*. All age references are intended to be approximate, for, as Burton White states: "Almost everyone who has studied young children agrees that one hallmark of early human development is variability. After all, children are not production-line products.[21]

Subsequently, literature sharing implications for library programs were derived from the early childhood literature information. These implications are for both informational programs for parents and caregivers of children under three years of age *and* storytimes for children under three years of age and are detailed in Chapter 4.

Five early childhood specialists located in New York City were asked, and kindly consented, to examine and review the schema. They included: Harriet Cuffaro of the Bank Street College of Education, Jeanna Gollobin of the Association for Parent Education of New York City, Irene Shigaki of the Leadership in Infant-Toddler

Care Program of New York University, Patricia Vardin
of the Early Childhood Education Program at Teachers
College, and Daniel Stern of the Payne Whitney Clinic,
author of *The First Relationship: Mother and Infant.*[22]
Personal consultations were arranged with these
specialists during which they gave their opinions about
the schema and offered suggestions for improvements.
Subsequent modifications in the schema reflected these
helpful suggestions.

Comparing the Schema with Practice in the Field

The final step in preparing an effective outline plan for
use by children's librarians was to compare the schema
with the actual practices and attitudes of librarians
actually engaged in conducting storytimes for children
under three and/or informational programs for parents and caregivers. With the assistance of children's
services consultants at state libraries, and others, and
information from library publications, 324 librarians
were identified to receive a questionnaire querying
their personal and institutional backgrounds, attitudes
toward library programs for children under three years
of age, and current practices in such programs.

The data from the returned survey questionnaires
were analyzed using a statistical analysis program.[23]

4

The Schema

An important goal for children's librarians is to instill a love for books in young children. While immediate objectives of introducing literature sharing activities to young children include aspects of language practice, listening and looking skills development, motor abilities of turning pages, and reinforcement of simple concepts, these objectives are not to be emphasized to such a degree that the pure enjoyment of books by the child is endangered. A loving adult who shares literature experiences with a young child provides that child with a feeling of security and a time for enjoyment. These pleasurable experiences may not only make *learning* to read an easier task for the child, but may form the basis for developing and sustaining a lifetime reading habit. Reaching the goal of enjoyment of and love for books includes the use of a variety of steps that can be made to correspond to the child's development.

The following schema is a compilation of early childhood development information from birth to three years of age with literature sharing implications which relate to library programs.

Since library programs are usually structured according to a chronological age range of children, this schema is organized into four growth periods from birth to three years of age. However, since human development deals with developmental rather than chronological age norms, literature sharing activities should be based on the child's developmental level. Even though characteristics of young children are identified here, the individual child passes through these stages at his or her own pace. All age references in this schema are intended to be average and approximate.

Birth to Six Months of Age

Early Childhood Development Information

Visual Exploration

- Shows elementary recognition of familiar objects without knowledge of their permanence.

- Stares at surroundings; stares at large or moving objects at a distance of several feet.

- At approximately three months, concentrates on a picture, toy, or other object either close-up or at a distance.

- Visually prefers people to objects; responds happily to faces.

- At approximately four months, vision approximates that of an adult; sees in color.

Tactile Exploration

- At approximately three months, begins to swipe at objects and to explore face, eyes, and mouth with hands.

- At approximately five months, eyes cooperate with hands in grasping and manipulating objects.

- Wants to touch, grasp, turn, and shake objects.

Oral Exploration

- Reaches for and tests orally things within grasp.

- Coos and hums using mostly vowel sounds.

Exploration by Listening *(receiving language)*

- At approximately one month, responds to a voice and may recognize a parent's voice.

- At approximately three months, distinguishes speech sounds and perceives syllable contrasts.

- Moves mouth and body rhythmically to adult speech that is directed to him or her.

- Turns head toward speaking or singing voices.

- At approximately five months, responds to human sounds more definitively; turns head, seems to look for the speaker.

- At approximately six months, may coo or stop crying on hearing music; reacts to change in volume; can imitate pitch.

Development of Trust and Dependency *(trust and the pleasure of dependency are conveyed by the caring person's embrace, comforting warmth, smile, way of talking to the infant, and also the quality of care)*

- Inner state becomes associated with consistent behavior of the caring person(s).

- At approximately six months, growing sense of belonging becomes evident (roots of identification).

Literature Sharing Implications for Library Programs

Since children in this age range—birth to approximately six months of age—usually are not able to directly benefit or participate in a *group* situation, library programs for these children should be informational programs directed at parents/caregivers, who can provide literature sharing experiences tailored to an individual infant. If a librarian offers storytimes for children of this age, the primary focus will probably be a "how to" demonstration for the parents/caregivers.

During *informational programs*, parents/caregivers should be encouraged to:

(1) Talk and sing to the newborn infant in a pleasant tone of voice, positioning the face close to the infant. When the infant coos, the adult repeats the sounds that he or she has made. As the infant gets

older (at approximately three to four months),
speaking and singing to the infant from different
areas of the room will encourage the baby to turn
around to look.

(2) Place large, clear pictures (especially those with
faces or high contrast) and mobiles in the infant's
environment. Pictures should be at his or her eye
level.

(3) Begin to show a visual variety of picture books to
the infant when he or she can focus on pictures (at
approximately four months). Durable books, such
as heavy cardboard books, are suggested. The
book should show large, clear pictures in bright
but real-life colors. The pictures should be of whole
objects, usually one to a page, and should realisti-
cally depict things that are in the infant's environment, such as familiar food, toys, and objects.

(4) Make simple books or individual pages by gluing
pictures of familiar objects, food, and animals to
heavy cardboard. The use of textured materials for
homemade books or pages is suggested since these
materials provide tactile as well as visual experiences for the infant.

(5) Play turn-taking games with the infant using
pictures, gestures, and sounds.

(6) Share picture books, sing songs, and tell nursery
rhymes when both adult and baby are relaxed,
the adult holding the baby. Do not extend the
book experience beyond the infant's interest and
enjoyment.

During *informational programs,* librarians should
provide practical guidance to sources and techniques
for parents/caregivers, such as:

(1) Presenting and discussing a varied selection of
picture books appropriate for children of this age.

(2) Presenting and discussing a selection of resource

books with literature sharing possibilities in the form of poetry, songs, and nursery rhymes.

(3) Demonstrating, as often as possible, "how to do" techniques (sharing a book with an infant) and "how to make" ideas (homemade books or pages) to parents/caregivers.

Seven Months to Fourteen Months of Age

Early Childhood Development Information

Language Development: Sounds

- At approximately seven months, has special, well-defined syllables (most common sounds like ma, mu, da, di, ba).

- Tries to imitate, combine, and repeat sounds or sound sequences.

- Listens to own vocalizations and those of others.

- At approximately nine months, intonation patterns become distinct; may say a syllable or a longer sequence repeatedly.

- May express a thought with a single word.

- Is aware that words are symbols for certain familiar objects: airplane, points to the sky; dog, growls.

- Jabbers with expression, reduplicating sounds that show emphasis and emotion.

- Attempts new words.

- At approximately fourteen months, is putting a variety of sounds together; enjoys the sounds of rhymes and jingles.

Language Development: Sentences
- At approximately eight months, babbles with a variety of sounds and inflections; begins to mimic mouth and jaw movements.

- At approximately ten months, understands and obeys words and simple commands, e.g., "Give it to me."

- May use jargon, sentences of gibberish in which meaningful words are sometimes embedded.

- Enjoys "conversations," especially turn-taking with words.

- At approximately fourteen months, babbles into a toy telephone; may say "bye-bye" to signify the end of the "conversation."

Learning Names of Objects *(environmental labeling)*
- At around seven months, attention is more concentrated; listens selectively to words of labels and tries to imitate sounds or sound sequences, i.e., cup, ball, book, etc.

- At approximately fourteen months, identifies some objects in his or her environment when asked, and some body parts when asked.

Development of Evocative Memory[1]
- Obtains an object behind a barrier; obtains a partially or slowly hidden object.

- Remembers segment representation of an entire situation.

- Remembers small series of actions in immediate past if series includes child's own behavior; at approximately nine months, retains small series of events in immediate past without child's own action.

- Begins showing memory of "timing" of routine events.

- At approximately twelve months, remembers events for longer and longer periods of time.

- Forms concept of person permanence; recognizes family members and other familiar people.

Development of Recognition of Mother and Father

- At approximately eight months, exhibits emotional attachment to caring person(s); when child becomes mobile approaches and follows caring person.

- May fear separation from parents (depending on child's previous social experiences).

Development of Curiosity *(need to explore)*[2]

- At approximately eight months, begins the crawling ability which aids so much in exploration.

- Examines objects as external three-dimensional realities.

- Uses one hand as holder, the other as explorer.

- At approximately twelve months, begins walking which greatly enlarges the ability to explore the environment.

- Through active trial and error, may find effective ways to solve problems.

- Explores in familiar area within eye-range of parent/caregiver; may exhibit routine of moving out to explore, coming back to parent/caregiver for reassurance, and moving out again.

- Is fascinated with his or environment; tries out movable parts in environment: light switches, television knobs, dials, etc.

- Use voluntary grasping ability to explore environment; turns objects over and over to observe reverse side.

- Enjoys collecting small objects and playing with them; explores notions of in-and-out or container-contained by putting small objects in and taking them out of a jar or other container.

Literature Sharing Implications for Library Programs

Since children in this age range—approximately seven months to fourteen months of age—are not yet likely to participate in a group situation, library programs for children of this age should be informational programs directed at parents/caregivers. If a librarian offers storytimes for children of this age, the primary focus will probably be a "how to" demonstration for the parents/caregivers.

During *informational programs,* parents/caregivers should be encouraged to:

(1) Respond to the child's babbles with conversation, and aid the child in putting new sounds together. The *sound* of language is important at this stage.

(2) Recite nursery rhymes to the child, and read and reread rhyming books to the child.

(3) Continue to show books to the child that have pictures of familiar objects. The technique in presenting these picture books includes pointing to and naming the object pictured, helping the child to recall any experiences with the real object; and, involving the child by asking him or her to repeat the name of the pictured object—a turn-taking technique.

(4) Assist the child in learning the skill of turning the pages of a picture book. At first the child may turn

more than one page at a time, but with help the child will learn the skill of turning one page at a time. With time and practice, the child will be able to manage without help.

(5) Continue to sing songs to and with the child.

(6) Show the child a real object along with a picture of the object, such as a ball, flower, or apple. Talk about the object and its use or qualities. The child is exposed to the relationship between pictures and reality, and the pictures become more meaningful. In time the child will realize that a two-dimensional picture represents a three-dimensional, real object.

(7) Look at picture books that have mother and father characters and pictures of people who can be equated with family members, such as "grandma." Show the child a photograph album that includes him or herself and family members.

(8) Point to and name objects in the child's environment.

(9) Ask the child to point to familiar objects and to parts of the body—e.g., eyes, ears, nose, feet—as they are named. Look at pictures of people and name the parts of their bodies.

(10) Read and reread books to the child. The child of this age enjoys repetition and familiarity.

(11) Engage in activities that involve the child, such as finger plays and creative dramatics. For example, after looking at a picture of a dog and talking about dogs, encourage the child to imitate a dog by crawling.

(12) Continue to provide tactile books (homemade or otherwise) for the child.

During *informational programs,* librarians should provide practical literature sharing ideas for parents/caregivers, such as:

(1) Presenting and discussing a varied selection of

picture books appropriate for children of this age.

(2) Presenting and discussing a selection of resource books with literature sharing ideas, such as poetry, song, finger play, and nursery rhyme books, and bibliographies.

(3) Demonstrating, as often as possible, "how to do" techniques (presenting stories using the pointing to and naming object technique, presenting finger plays, etc.) and "how to make" ideas (homemade tactile books, photograph albums, etc.) to parents/caregivers.

Fifteen Months to Twenty-Four Months of Age

Early Childhood Development Information

Development of New Motor Skills

- At approximately fifteen months, has discarded creeping and uses rapid running-like walk; enjoys climbing; wants to hold and carry objects in each hand.

- Likes to move to music; enjoys marching if directed.

- At approximately twenty-two months, jumps, runs, kicks, pushes and pulls, and throws; has increased smoothness of coordination in fine motor movements; turns pages of books with practice.

Language Development: New Words

- Intersperses babbling with real words.

- Imitates simple sounds on request.

- Enjoys question-and-answer games; when asked, points to most pictures of familiar objects.

- Understands much that is said to him or her.

- At approximately twenty months, repeatedly asks, "What's that?"; is discovering that everything has a name; is learning to label actions or qualities.

- Understands and uses word combinations, e.g., "all gone."

- Is interested in sounds and repetition; echoes adults' words and inflections.

- Combines words into sentences.

- At approximately twenty-four months, discards most jargon; actively imitates words.

Social Development[3]

- At approximately fifteen months, is more demanding and more self-assertive; demands personal attention; is definitely making a place as a member of the family.

- Is increasingly aware of "myself" as a separate person, with powers, potentials, and limitations.

- Recognizes the ownership of objects but does not yet understand the concept of sharing; tends to be egocentric (universe is centered upon himself or herself).

- Explores the effect he or she can have on other people, and learns that different people react in different ways.

- Is beginning to be able to sympathize with another person (can imagine to some extent the feelings of the other person).

- Associates persons with locations and locations with persons.

- Often tells of immediate experiences; is able to communicate feelings, desires, and interests to other people using words and gestures.

Exploration and Manipulation of Objects

- At approximately fifteen months, rubs fingers across a variety of surfaces, sorting out the textures that please, amuse, or displease.

- Likes to smell different odors.

- Enjoys manipulative play with experimentation; demonstrates understanding of "right side up."

- Enjoys push and pull toys, pile-up toys; explores cabinets, drawers, etc.; likes to turn on faucets.

- Enjoys water play and sand play.

- Is engrossed in take-apart toys; likes to fit things together, zips and unzips zippers.

- Combines toys in complex play.

- Parallel play predominates; tends not to be ready for cooperative play or activities.

- Solves puzzles that have a few pieces.

Staring Behavior

- Engages in long periods of looking at objects, people and environment.

Involvement with Primary Caregivers

- Looks for parent or caregiver when left alone; may experience anxiety of separation (depending on child's previous social experiences).

- Enjoys "helping" with housework.

Negativism *(beginning sense of autonomy)*

- Has shifting moods; temper, while quickly aroused, tends to be short-lived.

- Is struggling to be independent; is testing limits, as well as ability and right to have own say.

- At approximately eighteen months, may often oppose parents; practices the mastery of own autonomous capacities.

- At approximately twenty-four months, seems to be testing powers of self-assertion; wants own way in many things; sometimes challenges parent's desires.

Literature Sharing Implications for Library Programs

Library programs for children in this age range—approximately fifteen months to twenty-four months of age—can be directed as informational programs for parents/caregivers, and as storytimes.

During *informational programs,* parents/caregivers should be encouraged to:

(1) Continue to respond to the child's jargon in a conversational manner. Repeat and respond to words spoken by the child. Speak to the child in simple, short sentences, using adjectives and adverbs (with no "baby talk"). Give simple explanations in addition to commands; and, continue to tell the child the names of objects in the environment, such as the names of food, clothing, furniture, etc.

(2) Provide old gift catalogs and colorful magazines with which the child can practice turning pages. Imbued with a growing sense of autonomy, he or she will want to turn the pages without help.

(3) Begin to show books that have pictures which are more complex than those formerly used. For example, use pictures showing some type of action or relationship between two or more familiar objects. Point out the objects or let the child identify them; talk about the objects. Let the child "read" the pictures.

(4) Continue to provide visual variety in the child's environment. Place large, clear pictures showing some type of action or two or more objects on walls at the child's eye level.

(5) Provide a range of textures in the environment for the child to touch, including tactile books. In addition, provide books that involve exploration, such as manipulation books.

(6) Make simple puzzles that the child can manipulate with a few pieces of poster board.

(7) Involve the child in literature experiences that include participation, such as "show me the dog in the picture."

(8) Continue to sing songs together and to do finger plays together.

(9) Look at pictures in books that refer to and reinforce experiences the child has had. For example, after a visit to the zoo, look at a picture book about animals that were there; talk about the animals— what they look like, the sounds they make, the food they eat and how they react to the people.

(10) Continue to look at picture books with people who can be equated with family members, i.e., mothers, fathers, siblings. Look at photographs of the child and family members; and, talk about the people in the photo, where it was taken, and the action in the photo. Look at pictures that show families and their relationship to young children.

During *informational programs,* librarians should provide practical literature sharing ideas for parents/ caregivers, such as:

(1) Presenting and discussing a varied selection of picture books appropriate for children of this age.

(2) Presenting and discussing a selection of resource books with literature sharing ideas, such as poetry, song, finger play, exploration and manipulation, and nursery rhyme books and bibliographies.

(3) Demonstrating, as often as possible, "how to do" techniques (presenting pictures with action, presenting finger plays, etc.) and "how to make" ideas (pictures, homemade tactile books, simple puzzles, photograph albums) to parents/caregivers.

During *storytimes* for children of this age, the librarian should recognize that:

(1) The children may not "sit still" for the duration of the storytime, and that the storytime should be interspersed with activities that involve the children and allow them to move around. (The child's concept of "finished" may be different from the adult's.)
(2) Parents/caregivers should stay with children during the storytime to prevent possible anxiety of separation.
(3) Parents/caregivers should be encouraged to actively participate in the activities presented during the storytime, such as joining in doing finger plays and singing songs, in order to serve as models for their children to imitate.
(4) Even though the children are able to join in and do similar things together as a group such as clapping, singing, etc., they do not yet understand the concept of sharing and are not ready for cooperative activities with each other.
(5) The same librarian should conduct successive storytimes so that the children can associate a person with a location.
(6) Appropriate *activities for the storytimes* could include:
    (a) conducting simple finger plays for the children to practice new hand skills.
    (b) using simple picture books that also can be sung, such as *Hush Little Baby*, etc.
    (c) saying nursery rhymes and simple poems.

(d) including creative dramatics, such as crawling and meowing like cats, following a story about cats.

(e) using picture books about mothers, fathers, and other family members.

(f) showing a real object and then showing a picture of the object in a book, such as a flower or a ball.

(g) including flannel board activities, such as telling a simple story or singing a song while putting pictures of the characters or objects on the flannel board, for example, "Old McDonald."

(h) matching a few actions or sounds to some very uncomplicated picture books about experiences common to the children, such as going to the zoo or beach, seeing a fire truck, or taking a ride on a bus or train.

(i) including activities, such as songs, finger plays or flannel boards, about the parts of the body. For example, include a flannel board activity with a picture showing the parts of the body—the eyes, head, legs, arms, etc.—that can be placed on the board one part at a time.

(j) holding large, clear pictures that the children can look at during a poem or song.

(k) using simple puppets with activities, such as a black glove when singing the "Eency, Weency Spider."

Twenty-Five Months to
Thirty-Six Months of Age

Early Childhood Development Information

Language Development: Speaking in Sentences

- Begins to use expanded vocabulary in word combinations.

- Labels objects, people, emotions, sounds, etc.

- Accompanies much play with words and combinations of words, such as talking to a teddy bear when tucking it in for bedtime.

- Is able to talk about events of the day.

- Understands and uses texture words, such as rough, hard, soft; understands and uses abstract words, such as later, far, high.

- Is learning to rhyme words.

Pride in Personal Accomplishments: Growing Autonomy

- Is continuing the practice and mastery of autonomous capacities; wants to "do it myself"; is assuming an increasingly more self-sufficient attitude.

- At approximately twenty-six months, washes and dries own hands; attempts to undress self.

- Regardless of growing autonomy may still fear separation from parents (depending on child's previous social experiences).

- At approximately thirty-six months, shows self-control and a sense of self; within limits can wait to

take turn, but does not understand the concept of
sharing.

- Will play beside another child but has difficulty
with cooperative activities.

Development of Sense of Humor; Curiosity; Guessing

- At approximately twenty-five months, is actively
curious about animate and inanimate environment: people, small animals, birds, objects, places,
etc.

- Shows evidence of budding sense of humor; enjoys
"joking."

- At approximately thirty months, shows increasing
humor at surprises, harmless accidents, animal
actions, tricks, mistakes.

- Enjoys simple guessing games; loves to anticipate
"what comes next?"

- Shows interest in change; enjoys observing changes
in environment, for example, growing flowers, day
and night, weather, seasons, etc.

Imitation of Others and Symbolic Imitation

- Becomes involved in make-believe activities, such
as "dress-up" (is assuming the role of an adult by
putting on adult clothes, shoes, etc.), and role
playing, such as using "tools" used by an adult in
relation to an occupation.

- Transforms one object into another in play, such as
taking a block and pushing it, saying "car."

- Tells stories to an object such as a doll.

- Becomes involved in the process of shifting attention from self to others and then back again;

however, is still egocentric in thought, i.e., sees things from his or her point of view.

- Enjoys repetition of activities.

- Imitates animals, such as dogs or cats, and objects, such as cars or airplanes.

- Engages in imaginary play that involves pretending going to sleep, eating something, etc.

- Creates dramatic play with uncomplicated plots.

Ability to Deal with Simple Concepts

- Is able to sort objects with an idea in mind; will put things together, usually according to size or color.

- Names some colors.

- Learns to count, however, not necessarily number correspondence but rather object correspondence.

- Is able to say some ABCs (usually rote naming).

Literature Sharing Implications for Library Programs

Library programs for children in this age range—approximately twenty-five months to thirty-six months of age—can be directed as informational programs for parents/caregivers, and as storytimes.

During *informational programs*, parents/caregivers should be encouraged to:

(1) Provide an orderly and well-organized environment which stimulates the child with a variety of toys and books, and time for their use. Parents/caregivers play important roles in development at this age, especially concerning language development. Paying attention is important, especially in answering questions and in conversation.

(2) Continue to read story books with uncomplicated plots to the child. Story books with one picture per page and limited text with short sentences and repetition are suggested as beginning books. The story books should be short, and capable of being completed in one reading session. The pictures in the stories should continue to be colorful. The story character(s) should, in most cases, appear in several of the pages in the story so that the child becomes aware of the story sequence.

(3) Read stories slowly and clearly to allow the child time to assimilate the meaning of the words and to translate the pictures into the words that are being heard.

(4) Show enthusiasm with voice inflection when they read stories to the child, but not to the point that it distracts from the story.

(5) Read and reread a variety of types of story books to the child, including picture books, sensory books, books of nursery rhymes, story books with pictures, and homemade books.

(6) Reread stories that the child enjoys, such as:
   (a) make-believe stories.
   (b) short, funny stories that require turning one or more pages to learn how it ends.
   (c) stories that include change, such as day/night, growing things, weather, seasons, etc.
   (d) stories that include guessing or finding objects or characters.
   (e) rhyming stories.

(7) Read stories that the child can "read" independently after hearing them often. Many will enjoy "anticipating" (remembering) what happens on the next page—especially a sound such as the animals make or the repetition of Danny's "No thank you" in *Ask Mr. Bear*.

(8) Involve the child with the story activity. Let the child select the books he or she wants to share, and

become involved by turning the pages. Ask questions about the pictures, and encourage the child to talk about his or her own experiences and feelings as they relate to the story.

(9) Share books with their child often. Establish a routine time and place for reading together, in addition to on the spur of the moment reading times. Let the child sit in the parent's/caregiver's lap during a one-to-one story. Remember, however, to keep book activities short. Do not turn literature sharing experiences into long, tiring sessions.

(10) Introduce basic concept books—such as ABC, color, size and shape, and number books—to the child. The child needs exposure to letters and numbers. These are abstract symbols to the child that will come to have meaning with the passage of time and experience.

(11) Many stories and related activities lend themselves to use of a flannel board when the story is reread or retold by the parent/caregiver or the child. The librarian should demonstrate how to make a flannel board out of heavy cardboard covered with flannel. Story characters and objects drawn on and cut out of felt or other materials, or pictures from magazines, can be used by securing strips of sandpaper to the back of the pictures so that they adhere to the flannel board. As a character or object appears in the story, the child can place the figure on the flannel board. The child must listen carefully to know when the characters and objects appear in the story, so this activity also develops listening skills.

(12) Let the child see them reading. Parents/caregivers serve as models for their children. Parents/caregivers should also reinforce the idea that children are becoming readers, and that that is something exciting and wonderful to be.

(13) Provide musical activities since they tend to include both assimilative and accommodative

functions. The child's own music-making may be assimilative, while the learning of songs involves accommodations to pitch, rhythm, and words. Songs and rhymes familiarize the child with numerical and other ideas, e.g., "Three Little Kittens," or "The Alphabet Song."

(14) Since most children have and express preferences, be patient when the child repeatedly asks for the same story or activity, such as a finger play, over and over. Children of this age enjoy repetition of stories; familiarity often increases enjoyment.

(15) Visit their public library on a regular basis. The child will enjoy the outing, the change in environment and the idea of an adventure with a special adult. Such visits reinforce the social aspects of books and reading. Let the *child* select some books to take home in addition to the books selected by the parent/caregiver.

During *informational programs,* librarians should provide practical literature sharing ideas for parents/caregivers, such as:

(1) Presenting and discussing a varied selection of picture books appropriate for children of this age.

(2) Presenting and discussing a selection of resource books with literature sharing ideas, such as poetry, song, finger play, nursery rhyme books, and bibliographies.

(3) Demonstrating, as often as possible, "how to do" techniques (finger plays, sharing picture books) and "how to make" ideas (flannel board and figures for flannel board use, homemade books) to parents/caregivers.

During *storytimes* for children of this age, librarians should recognize that:

(1) Children of this age are very active. Continue to intersperse the storytime with activities that

involve the children, such as finger plays, creative dramatics, etc.

(2) Parents/caregivers should stay with their children during the storytime to prevent possible anxiety of separation.

(3) Parents/caregivers should be encouraged to actively participate in the activities presented during the storytime, such as finger plays and songs, because parents/caregivers serve as models for their children. In addition, parents/caregivers are able to present follow-up activities and repeat portions of the storytime since children enjoy the repetition of stories and activities.

(4) Parents/caregivers should be provided with details about the books and activities, such as booklists or printed handouts of finger plays, poems, etc., either before or following the storytime so that the stories and activities can be repeated with the children later.

(5) Even though the children can take turns and are able to join in and do similar things together, such as finger plays, clapping, creative dramatics, etc., they do not yet understand the concept of sharing and are not ready for cooperative activities.

(6) The same librarian should conduct successive storytimes so that the children can associate a person with a location.

(7) Appropriate *activities for the storytimes* could include:

    (a) stories that have simple plots, large, clear pictures, and limited text with short sentences and repetition.

    (b) pretend stories and activities.

    (c) funny stories that require turning one or more pages to learn how the story ends.

    (d) stories and activities that involve change, such as day/night, growing things, weather, seasons, etc.

(e) stories and activities that involve guessing.

(f) rhyming stories and nursery rhymes, along with simple poems.

(g) related visuals, such as simple puppets and large, clear pictures for poems, songs, etc., that the children can look at during the activity.

(h) a variety of flannel board stories and activities.

(i) more complex finger plays and creative dramatics.

(j) musical activities, including songs, marching, etc.

(k) stories and activities about topics that are familiar to the child, such as food, play, family, animals, trains and cars, parts of the body, and familiar places.

(l) stories and activities that introduce simple concepts, such as sizes and shapes, colors, numbers, ABCs.

The library activities I have given here, inspired by and related to the developmental characteristics in the four categories, will be just a starting point, a springboard, for children's librarians. Creative practitioners will study the early childhood characteristics given and make up their own activities and find materials that are tailored to the needs and interests of the young children with whom they are working.

5

Description of Librarians
in the Study

One of the reasons for sending the questionnaire based on the schema was to ascertain librarians' practices and attitudes, and to see how these related to institutional and personal characteristics. Of the 324 librarians who received the questionnaire, 253 responded. The population consisted of those librarians who offered either or both of the following early childhood literature sharing programs: (1) storytimes for children under three years of age, and (2) informational programs for parents and/or caregivers of children under three years of age. (See Appendix A for a copy of the questionnaire.)

The participants were geographically widely distributed throughout the country with the New England Region having the largest proportion (23%) of programs. See the map entitled "Geographical Distribution of Participants" for a complete distribution of participants by state and by regional boundaries (indicated with heavy black lines).

Institutional Characteristics

The information gathered revealed that two-fifths (40%) of the librarians queried were children's librarians in a main library or a library with no branches; about one-third (35%) were supervisors or heads of children's services in their libraries; less than one-fifth (17%) were children's librarians in a branch library; and the remaining 8% were classified "other." The majority (53%) of librarians worked in libraries that served suburban areas, while 30% worked in urban areas, 15% in rural areas, and 3% in a combination of types of areas.

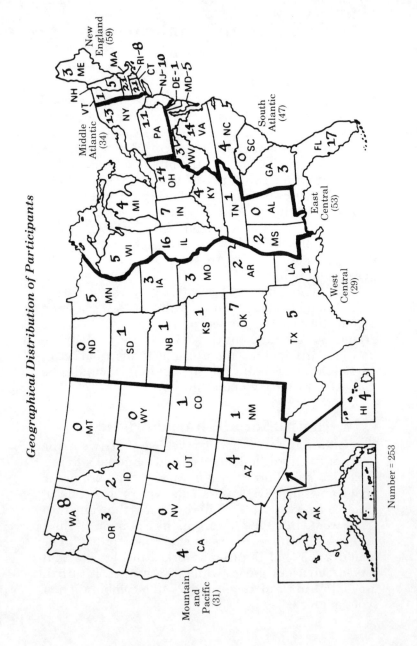

Geographical Distribution of Participants

New England (59)
NH — 3
ME
VT — 1
MA — 5
RI — 8
CT — 2
NJ — 10
DE — 1
MD — 5

Middle Atlantic (34)
NY — 13
PA — 11

South Atlantic (47)
VA — 14
WV — 3
NC — 4
SC — 0
GA — 3
FL — 17

East Central (53)
OH — 14
MI — 4
IN — 7
IL — 16
WI — 5
KY — 4
TN — 1
AL — 0
MS — 2

West Central (29)
IA — 3
MO — 3
MN — 5
ND — 0
SD — 1
NB — 1
KS — 1
OK — 7
TX — 5
AR — 2
LA — 1

Mountain and Pacific (31)
MT — 0
WY — 0
CO — 1
NM — 1
ID — 2
UT — 2
AZ — 4
WA — 8
OR — 3
NV — 0
CA — 4
HI — 4
AK — 2

Number = 253

The number of full-time children's librarians in the participants' libraries varied greatly from none to over fourteen full-time children's librarians. The most common number of children's librarians was one (53%), followed by those having 2 to 3 children's librarians (20%). It is interesting to note that although 10% of the participants reported that they did not have a full-time children's librarian in their libraries, they offered early childhood literature sharing programs.

In addition, the size of the budget for children's materials and programming varied greatly; however, the largest proportion of librarians had a budget from $5,000 to $12,000 during 1981. Only a small proportion (15%) of the participants received any type of grant funding for the programs in question. Likewise, a relatively small proportion (17%) reported that outside consultants were used in designing their programs. For those libraries where consultants were used, the most common types of outside consultants were other children's librarians (23%), early childhood specialists (19%), state library personnel (16%), people from community agencies (14%), and a combination of the above (14%).

Personal Characteristics

Questions about certain personal background characteristics were also asked. The length of service as a children's librarian varied from less than one year to over nineteen years of experience. The most frequent was from 4 to 6 years of service (28%) followed by from 10 to 12 years of service (21%).

Among the librarians responding, the majority (68%) held a master's degree in library science (MLS). The next largest proportion (17%) held a bachelor's degree which was in most cases in elementary education.

It is interesting that a large proportion (41%) of the librarians had previously been classroom or nursery school teachers. However, of these, only 22% had been teachers of children under five years of age. The librarians were nearly equally divided in their status as parents, 55% being parents.

Participants were asked to indicate their training for working with children under age three. It is impressive and significant to note that 43% of the respondents had taken formal courses in early childhood education. However, only a small proportion (8%) had a specialization or degree in this field.

Respondents were also asked how many books or articles concerning early childhood development they had read during the previous one-year period. A majority (54%) had read from 1 to 10 books or articles; 36% had read from 11 to 25; and 8% read more than 25. Only 2% reported that they had not read any books or articles concerning early childhood development during that time period.

Queried as to which professional organization, if any, they had memberships in, a very large majority (90%) of the participants said they belonged to at least one professional organization. The most common organization was their state library association (82%), followed by the American Library Association (ALA) (46%) and Association for Library Service to Children (ALSC) a division of ALA (32%). A relatively small but noteworthy number of participants held memberships in early childhood education organizations. Twenty-five (10%) belonged to a national early childhood education organization, the most common being the National Association for the Education of Young Children (NAEYC); and, 22 (9%) belonged to a pre-school organization in their local area.

Description of the Programs Provided

Background information concerning the programs the librarians offered was also gathered. A very large proportion (93%) offered storytimes for children under three years of age, and nearly one-half (49%) of the participants offered informational programs for parents and/or caregivers of such children. Respondents who offered only one kind of program, that is, storytimes or informational programs, were queried about their reason for not offering the other kind, and it is interesting that in the case of both storytimes and informational programs the largest proportion of respondents reported their reason to be a shortage of staff.

Since programs of this nature are comparatively innovative types of library services, it is not surprising that a vast majority (87%) of the storytimes as well as a large proportion (69%) of the informational programs were begun within the five year period prior to the survey.

The age range of children for whom the participants' storytimes were designed varied greatly. However, the most frequent (51%) age range was for children from 24 months to 36 months of age, followed by 18 months to 36 months (20%). The age range of children for whose parents and adult caregivers the participants' informational programs were designed also varied greatly. Forty-nine percent reported that their informational programs were designed for parents/caregivers of children from birth to 36 months of age (or older), followed by 20% who designed programs for children from 24 months to 36 months (or older).

Participants who offered informational programs were queried about their audiences—parents and/or caregivers. The majority (76%) reported that they offered programs for both parents and caregivers. Twenty-two percent offered programs only to parents, and 2% only to caregivers.

6
Analysis of the Data

Ninety-three percent of the librarians in the study offered storytimes, and they were queried about their storytime practices. These practices in turn were compared to statements that were made in the schema. If responses were in agreement with the schema, they were corresponding; and if responses were in disagreement with the schema, they were noncorresponding.

The data suggest that the practices of children's librarians overwhelmingly correspond to the schema as far as storytime practices are concerned. For example, 91% of the librarians who offered storytimes on a regularly scheduled basis maintained the practice of having the same librarian conduct the storytimes for the duration of the series; 5% sometimes held to that practice while 4% did not. The schema, you will recall, advises the same librarian should conduct successive storytimes so that young children can associate a person with a location.

It is also stated in the schema that parents/caregivers should stay with their young children during storytimes to prevent any anxiety of separation that could occur. An additional advantage to this, of course, is that parents/caregivers are exposed to the books and activities presented during the storytimes and this can help them in literature sharing experiences with their young children at home, or at other sites. Of the 235 librarians who offered storytimes, 91% reported that parents and caregivers stayed with their young children during the storytimes, 6% reported that the choice was left to the parent/caregiver and 3% reported they did not require them to stay.

The 214 participants who responded that parents/caregivers stayed with their young children during the storytimes were asked if they encouraged parents/

caregivers to participate actively with their children in the activities presented during the storytimes. The schema indicates that parents/caregivers *should* be encouraged to participate with their children in the activities since in that way they may serve as models for their young children to imitate. Additionally, parents/caregivers are able to present follow-up activities and repeat portions of the storytimes at a later time with the children. A very large proportion, 97%, reported that they encouraged parents and caregivers to participate with their children in the activities presented during storytimes, once again placing the librarian's practice in correspondence to the schema.

The 125 librarians who offered informational programs were queried about their informational program practices, and, as in the case of the storytime practices, the data suggest that the existing practice is in close correspondence with the schema. For example, the schema suggests that during informational programs, storytime techniques (such as finger plays, how to use a flannel board, etc.) suitable for children under three years of age should be demonstrated to parents/caregivers. Among the participants who offered informational programs, 74% reported that they demonstrated storytime techniques, 19% reported that they sometimes demonstrated them, and only 7% reported that they did not provide this type of guidance.

The schema advises that during informational programs librarians should show parents/caregivers a selection of resource books (books with finger plays, songs, poetry, and bibliographies) with literature sharing ideas for young children. Responses to this query given by participants who offered informational programs were in high correspondence to the schema with 89% reporting that they provided resource books, 10% reporting that they sometimes offered them, and only 1% reporting they did not provide them.

Respondents were also asked if they showed parents/caregivers a selection of books appropriate for children under three years of age during their informational programs, which is a suggested practice in the schema. It is interesting to note that all of the study's respondents either did provide (92%) or sometimes provided (8%) this stimulus and encouragement to parents and caregivers.

Librarians in the survey were queried also about their attitudes to determine whether they corresponded to the recommendations of the schema.

In order to arrive at any conclusions, the 253 survey participants were asked their opinions about certain statements that were made in the schema. The questionnaire contained two attitudinal sections.

The first section consisted of twenty-four statements[1] with which participants were asked to indicate their level of agreement according to the following scale:

(1) Strongly Agree

(2) Somewhat Agree

(3) No Opinion

(4) Somewhat Disagree

(5) Strongly Disagree

Some queries in the survey were not in correspondence with the schema, and these statements are marked with two asterisks:

(1) The development of a love for books is the most important goal of library programs for children under three years of age.

(2) Since parents/caregivers serve as models, children under three years of age should see them reading.

(3) Homemade books with various textured materials should be suggested to parents for use by their young children.

(4) Storytimes for children under three years of age should include activities that involve the child.

(5) It is important for young children to hear the sound of language.

(6) Parents or caregivers should stay with children under three years of age during library storytimes.

(7) The same librarian should conduct an entire series of storytimes for children under three years of age.

(8) Parents should be encouraged to repeat storytime activities at home with their young children.

(9) Parents and caregivers of infants should place large, clear pictures with high contrast in the infant's environment.

(10) Parents and caregivers should provide magazines with which the child can practice turning pages.

(11) Visiting the public library should be a routine that is established early in a child's life.

(12) Children under three years of age have limited imaginations and do *not* enjoy "make believe" stories.**

(13) Children under three years of age benefit from seeing a real object along with a picture of it in a story.

(14) After hearing a story, children under three years of age can cooperatively act it out with other children their age.**

(15) Infants learn by using their senses: looking, listening, smelling, and touching.

(16) Nursery rhymes are inappropriate for children under three years of age.**

(17) Children under three years of age are very egocentric; they believe that the world revolves around themselves.

(18) Children under three years of age do *not* yet fully understand the concept of sharing and are *not* yet ready for cooperative activities.

(19) Children under three years of age have the ability to listen to a simple story and create new endings to the story.**

(20) Children between two and three years of age are frustrated by guessing games.**

(21) When a child nears his/her third birthday, he/she is ready for books which introduce simple concepts, such as numbers, colors, ABCs, or sizes and shapes.

(22) Children under three years of age enjoy stories and activities that involve changes, such as day/night, weather, growing things, etc.

(23) Children under three years of age are ready for stories that will take several reading sessions to complete.**

(24) Photograph albums with snapshots of family members are enjoyable to a child under three years of age.

According to the schema all but statements 12, 14, 16, 19, 20 and 23—those shown with the (**) notation—were true and appropriate statements. It was judged that if participants indicated either level of agreement (strongly agree or somewhat agree), to statements that were included in the schema, the responses were corresponding. These included statements 1-11, 13, 15, 17, 18, 21, 22, and 24 in the above list. In addition, if participants indicated a level of disagreement to statements that were *not* appropriate and therefore were *not* included in the schema, those responses were also considered to be corresponding. These included statements 12, 14, 16, 19, 20 and 23 in the above list.

Noncorrespondence was determined similarly. If participants indicated a level of disagreement to statements which were included as being true in the schema, the responses were noncorresponding; and, if they indicated a level of agreement to statements which were inappropriate and *not* included in the schema, the responses were likewise noncorresponding.

A summary of the participants' responses to the 24 statements is presented in Table 1. As shown, abbreviated labels for the statements are used, followed by the number of librarians who responded to the statement. The five categories indicating the level of agreement or disagreement are also provided with the number and percentage of participants who responded to each category. Since there was a five point scale of agreement, the mean of responses to each statement is also given.

By and large, respondents had opinions one way or the other about the statements, demonstrated by the fact that the largest proportion of no-opinion answers to any of the 24 statements was only 25%. This was to statement 20, "children between two to three years of age are frustrated by guessing games."

In order to reduce the data and provide an overall picture, a composite variable, or index, was constructed from the attitudinal variables in the first section of the survey. This index was created to illustrate the participants' responses to all 24 statements as compared to the schema.

As previously mentioned, the statements in the questionnaire were derived from the schema. Some of the statements were in the negative in the questionnaire; and, therefore, these statements were not in correspondence to the schema. In the case of the statements which were not in agreement to the schema, the values were reversed for calculation of the index.

On a scale from 1—which is total correspondence to the schema—to 5—which is absence of correspondence to the schema—the mean of the "Index of Attitudes" was 1.7, indicating a high level of correspondence to the schema. Figure 1 presents a distribution of means of the index. The largest proportion (12% or 28) of participants had a mean of 1.8, followed by 11% (26) having a mean of 1.6. The means of the 233 participants had a range of 1.14, from a high mean of 1.23 to a low mean of 2.37.

In the case of the second attitudinal section, which consisted of three queries with a choice of two possible

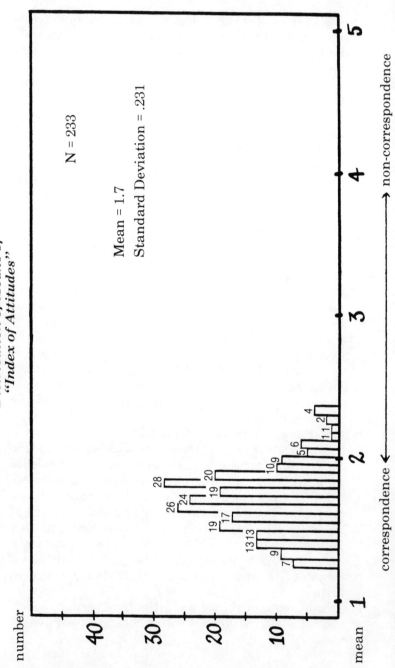

Figure 1
Distribution of Means of
"Index of Attitudes"

N = 233

Mean = 1.7
Standard Deviation = .231

Table 1
Responses to Individual Attitude Statements

Statement	Number	Strongly Agree (1)	Somewhat Agree (2)	No Opinion (3)	Somewhat Disagree (4)	Strongly Disagree (5)	Mean
1. love for books	248	108 (44%)	97 (40%)	1 (*)	35 (14%)	7 (3%)	1.935
2. serve as models	251	229 (92%)	20 (8%)	1 (*)	0	1 (*)	1.104
3. textured materials	249	154 (62%)	61 (25%)	31 (12%)	3 (1%)	0	1.530
4. activities that involve	251	228 (91%)	19 (7%)	1 (*)	3 (1%)	0	1.120
5. sound of language	252	245 (97%)	7 (3%)	0	0	0	1.028
6. p/c stay	251	186 (74%)	46 (18%)	8 (3%)	7 (3%)	4 (2%)	1.394

continued

Table 1
(continued)

Statement	Number	Strongly Agree (1)	Somewhat Agree (2)	No Opinion (3)	Somewhat Disagree (4)	Strongly Disagree (5)	Mean
7. same librarian conducts	251	155 (62%)	66 (26%)	13 (5%)	14 (6%)	3 (1%)	1.582
8. parents repeat	252	218 (87%)	28 (11%)	5 (2%)	1 (*)	0	1.163
9. p/c place pictures	252	146 (58%)	70 (28%)	34 (13%)	2 (1%)	0	1.571
10. p/c provide magazines	251	102 (41%)	78 (31%)	56 (22%)	13 (5%)	2 (1%)	1.944
11. library routine	251	241 (96%)	10 (4%)	0	0	0	1.040
12. do NOT enjoy "make believe" (**)	249	9 (4%)	42 (17%)	13 (5%)	63 (25%)	122 (49%)	3.992

Table 1
(continued)

Statement	Number	Strongly Agree (1)	Somewhat Agree (2)	No Opinion (3)	Somewhat Disagree (4)	Strongly Disagree (5)	Mean
13. object with picture	251	126 (50%)	93 (37%)	25 (10%)	5 (2%)	2 (1%)	1.661
14. cooperatively act out (**)	249	12 (5%)	69 (28%)	33 (13%)	86 (34%)	49 (20%)	3.365
15. learn by senses	252	236 (94%)	14 (5%)	2 (1%)	0	0	1.071
16. rhymes inappropriate (**)	252	5 (2%)	3 (1%)	2 (1%)	21 (8%)	221 (88%)	4.786
17. egocentric	247	151 (61%)	75 (30%)	9 (4%)	9 (4%)	3 (1%)	1.534
18. do NOT understand sharing	250	41 (17%)	86 (34%)	11 (4%)	70 (28%)	42 (17%)	2.944
19. create new endings (**)	250	29 (12%)	80 (32%)	57 (23%)	59 (23%)	25 (10%)	2.884

continued

Table 1
(continued)

Statement	Number	Strongly Agree (1)	Somewhat Agree (2)	No Opinion (3)	Somewhat Disagree (4)	Strongly Disagree (5)	Mean
20. frustrated by guessing (**)	250	20 (8%)	58 (23%)	61 (25%)	80 (32%)	31 (12%)	3.176
21. simple concepts	250	132 (53%)	84 (33%)	7 (3%)	15 (6%)	12 (5%)	1.764
22. involve changes	248	114 (46%)	102 (41%)	22 (9%)	7 (3%)	3 (1%)	1.722
23. several sessions (**)	251	2 (1%)	4 (2%)	12 (5%)	67 (26%)	166 (66%)	4.558
24. photo albums	250	117 (47%)	74 (30%)	49 (19%)	10 (4%)	0	1.808

(*) less than .5% but more than 0
(**) statement does not correspond to the Schema

responses, the level of agreement between the participants' attitudes and the schema was astoundingly high. For example, 99.6% indicated that a child's *developmental age* not a child's chronological age is a better indicator of appropriate stories for the child. The schema states that the developmental age is a better indicator. The second query had nearly as high a level of correspondence to the schema. Ninety-five percent reported they believe that children under three years of age *do* have book preferences. And, as in the case of the two previous questions, there existed a high degree of correspondence to the schema on the librarians' part to the third query. Only one participant gave a noncorresponding response, while 99.6% indicated they are of the opinion that children under three years of age *enjoy,* as opposed to dislike, repetition of stories.

The conclusion to which examination of the data led is that the attitudes as well as the practices, of librarians who offer early childhood literature sharing programs, for the most part, correspond to the schema.

The survey was designed to show also whether the literature sharing practices and attitudes of librarians are independent of their institution's characteristics and their own backgrounds. These institutional and personal characteristics included the geographical region of the library, position of the librarian, type of community served, number of full-time children's librarians, size of budget, length of service, level of education, past teaching experience, parental status, courses that had been taken in early childhood education, amount of early childhood development reading, professional organization memberships, when storytimes began, age range of children for storytimes, when informational programs began, and more.

Results indicate that not only do the literature sharing practices and attitudes of librarians who participated in this study correspond to the schema, but that the practices are independent of the librarians' institutional and personal characteristics. The attitudes of librarians, to a much lesser extent than the practices, were also independent of background varia-

bles. Variables which appeared to affect attitudes
included: (1) "if grant funding for early childhood
programs was received"; (2) "if librarian has past
classroom or nursery school teaching experience"; (3)
"if librarian has taken early childhood education
courses"; (4) "librarian's amount of early childhood
development reading"; and (5) "if librarian offers
informational programs for parents/caregivers." It is
important to note that the attitudes for librarians who
did receive grant funding, who *had* past teaching experience, who *had* taken early childhood education courses
who read *more*, and who *did* offer informational programs were more closely in agreement to the schema. (See Appendix B for analysis of variance tables.)

One could look at these five significant background
variables, and speculate why they appeared. If a
librarian received grant funding for early childhood
programs, he or she would most likely have to read
early childhood development literature to prepare for
the grant. A frequency distribution shows that this is in
fact the case: Librarians who received grant funding
read proportionately more early childhood development information. It would also be logical to assume
that librarians who had completed coursework in early
childhood education would have read proportionately
more just as those who were past teachers would, since
they are aware of the early childhood development literature. Frequency distributions again show that this
is the case. (See Appendix B for contingency tables.)

One could conclude, assuming that this study is
valid, that librarians who offer early childhood literature sharing programs are indeed practicing in their
programs what early childhood development information indicates they should be practicing. By and large,
their attitudes concerning early childhood programs
also correspond to early childhood development information, the correspondence being proportionately
higher for those who read more early childhood
development information.

7

The Programs:
Details and Comments

There were many interesting bits of information gathered via the questionnaire about early childhood literature sharing programs. This chapter includes details about the types of activities or topics that are included in storytimes or informational programs, which were not included in the schema and therefore were not a part of the analysis of the data. It also provides a selection from the comments made on the backs of questionnaires by the librarians who participated in the survey and an outline of some typical early childhood literature sharing programs.

Details of Storytimes and Informational Programs

The questionnaire provided a list with eleven general types of activities and librarians were asked to indicate the frequency of inclusion of the activities during their storytimes. Table 2 provides a breakdown of the responses. There are no surprises here. Nearly all respondents (95%) reported that they always included the standard activity of "simple stories" during their storytimes. Likewise, it is not surprising that only 1% included "puppet shows," an activity which is not very appropriate for children under three years of age.

In addition to the activities provided for selection in the question, librarians were given the opportunity to write in other types of activities they used. Table 3 provides an interesting list of "other" activities reported by librarians. The most widely used "other" activity was a "short film or filmstrip"; "simple arts and crafts" also was high on the list.

Table 2
Activities Included during Storytimes
with Their Frequency of Inclusion

Activity	Never or Seldom	Sometimes	Always
simple stories	0 (0%)	11 (5%)	226 (95%)
finger plays	11 (5%)	41 (17%)	185 (78%)
songs	23 (10%)	90 (38%)	124 (52%)
nursery rhymes	16 (7%)	156 (66%)	65 (27%)
musical activities	55 (23%)	112 (47%)	70 (30%)
simple puppets	46 (19%)	127 (54%)	64 (27%)
flannel or felt board stories	52 (22%)	134 (57%)	51 (21%)
simple poems	42 (18%)	163 (69%)	32 (13%)
creative dramatics	109 (46%)	113 (48%)	15 (6%)
marching activities	107 (45%)	119 (50%)	11 (5%)
puppet shows	169 (71%)	66 (28%)	2 (1%)

N = 237

Table 3
Additional Activities Listed by
Librarians in "Other"

Activity	Number
short film or filmstrip	54
simple arts and crafts	52
simple circle games	14
realia	13
snacks or refreshments	11
movement to music	8
informal playtime	5
tell and draw stories	5
concept games	4
study prints or pictures	4
participation stories	3
common objects (pots and pans, blocks) for play	3
tactile objects	2
special holiday activities	2
dress-up activities	2
stretching activities	2
bean bag games	2
waterplay activities	1
motor skill activities	1
manipulative materials	1
tasting, touching, smelling activities	1
ball rolling	1
puzzles	1
transparencies	1

N = 104

The librarians who offered storytimes were queried about the topics they included in their storytimes. A limited list, consisting of the following topics, was provided for their selection: (1) the parts of the body; (2) familiar places (zoo, beach, etc.); (3) the family; (4) play; (5) pretend activities; (6) common animals; (7) trains, cars, planes; (8) dinosaurs; and (9) superheroes. Table 4 provides a breakdown of the responses. The most common topic included in storytimes was "common animals" followed by "the family." Two topics, dinosaurs and superheroes, were deliberately included in the list even though they are generally considered unsuitable topics for children under three years of age.[1] A very large proportion of the respondents also believed them to be unsuitable.

Participants who offered informational programs were queried about practices they suggested to parents/caregivers of children under three years of age during their programs. A limited list, consisting of the following seven practices, was provided for their selection:

(1) Place large clear pictures in the child's environment.
(2) Show the child photograph albums with snap-shots of family members.
(3) Read stories that will take several reading sessions to complete.
(4) Sit the child on their laps during a one-to-one story.
(5) Provide old gift catalogs and colorful magazines which the child can use.
(6) Visit their public library on a regular basis.
(7) Provide the child with a variety of books including tactile books.

Table 5 provides a breakdown of responses reported by the 125 participants who offered informational programs. It is interesting to note that very few (only

Table 4
Which Topics are Included in Storytimes?

| Topic | Number of Librarians (percentage) | |
	Yes	No
parts of body	182 (77%)	54 (23%)
familiar places	207 (88%)	29 (12%)
the family	220 (93%)	16 (7%)
play	176 (75%)	60 (25%)
pretend activities	166 (70%)	70 (30%)
common animals	229 (97%)	7 (3%)
trains, cars, planes	189 (80%)	47 (20%)
dinosaurs	22 (9%)	214 (91%)
superheroes	8 (3%)	228 (97%)

N = 236

Table 5
Which Practices are Suggested
to Parents/Caregivers?

	Number of Librarians (percentage)	
Topic	Yes	No
place pictures	81 (65%)	44 (35%)
show photo albums	34 (27%)	91 (73%)
read long stories	6 (5%)	119 (95%)
sit on laps	111 (89%)	14 (11%)
provide magazines	56 (45%)	69 (55%)
visit library	118 (94%)	7 (6%)
provide book variety	104 (83%)	21 (17%)

N = 125

5%) of the librarians suggested the practice of "reading stories that will take several reading sessions to complete." Early childhood literature also suggests this is an inappropriate practice.

Comments from Librarians

The back page of the questionnaire booklet provided space for comments from the respondents. Some comments indicate the concerns of librarians who offer early childhood literature sharing programs; some comments offer how-to information; and others provide opinions about education, the value of the programs, and other matters.

> I think this is a new and important part of library service. This age group is ready to get together, but often has no organized way of doing so.

> Programming for two-year-olds has been very well received—the demand is overwhelming. The biggest obstacle which had to be overcome was reluctance of staff members to include two-year-olds, mainly based on their lack of experience with and their fear of this age group.

> I feel strongly that MLS programs do not produce competent children's librarians because they do not expose candidates to developmental theory or employ competency standards which focus on the interaction between librarians and children. I am encouraged by several articles in professional journals which express the same point of view.

> Not having had any experience with children under three, I was very uncertain at the outset of the programs I am working with. Other than being a mother of three children, I had little real knowledge of the "academic" needs of the toddler. I have come to love these children and their marvelous mothers (fathers attend infrequently). I have learned a great deal through classes,

personal reading and on-the-job experiences. I feel that this is probably the most exciting, reachable time of these children's lives. How exciting to play even a small part in their development!

I found that the response of parents to toddler programs in my area is very positive; there is definitely a need for and a response to this type of programming.

In my personal opinion library services for under threes should be with adults. The rewards of parent/child relationships at this age is invaluable—this relationship can be supported outside the home but acted out in the home with a lot of fun and love.

We offer a variety of programs for children under the age of three—a language development program, a learning/discovery program, various 'make-a-book' programs, etc. In addition, cooperative programs with other agencies and schools working with very young children and their parents/caregivers should be mentioned. In all instances, the scope of the library's activities with very young children must relate to the collection of appropriate materials for this age and for involved adults. I should also say that relevant research used in building our programs has been drawn primarily from fields outside library science.

Working with two-year-olds and their parents has been one of the most rewarding experiences. It has been an exciting focus point for my past educational and personal experiences.

My two-year-old storytime is the most challenging and worthwhile storytime I conduct. It is extremely beneficial to the parents who accompany the children because they learn so much from it; 95% of them continue to bring their child to the three-, four-, and five-year-old sessions later on. A marvelous introduction to the library and books at an early age.

Programming for children under age three is one of the most important aspects of my work. It is essential.

It is an enjoyable experience and a continual learning experience. We've had dads, grandparents, and lots of bit older and younger siblings. They are welcome. At first I thought this should be a 'special time' for just the parent and child, but that was not realistic when we are hoping to encourage parents to repeat these activities at home with all the distractions. And, it would limit attendance to those who could afford child care or could work out some cooperative effort. We do put out a selection of possible book choices as it is sometimes difficult to pick out books suitable just for toddlers with so much "help" around.

Our under-three story hours were started at the request of parents—and out of desperation. They were reducing my three- to four-year-olds' story hours to shambles. Workshops were spinoffs and given at the request of various agencies who heard about the program through word of mouth. They have been shaped largely by the type of material requested. The major difference in work with below threes as opposed to above threes is a difference in expectations of listener performance, and the use of materials.

Expectations of a two-year-old need to be different. The group needs to be small so eye contact is maximum because attention span is short. They need opportunity to talk and to move. Not all will participate. An alphabet book from A to Z is too much usually. More than 20 minutes is too long unless the story hour includes doing puzzles or individual browsing or reading. But neither should they be underestimated. They are capable of doing some of our most complex puzzles. With some experience they are capable of listening to three stories without a break for fingerplay or song. Their verbal and social skills vary immensely, but most are able to gain from story hour.

My basic commitment is making parents of young children feel *welcome* to bring their children to the library—aisles are wide enough for strollers, there is a changing sofa at the inner entrance to the women's restroom, and two sofas in the children's room for

"laptime with books," a mirror at toddler wall height
with indestructable hand puppets nearby. Periodically
posters are posted at toddler height. Our current goal is
to develop a much broader record and tape recording
collection for this group.

Our toddler story program also is aimed at getting
parents familiar with good children's books as well as
showing that the library is able to offer fun and
information. Since we began the program, our circula-
tion had increased overall. Families have gotten into
the habit of visiting the library, and they look for more
than books for and about their children. They've been
exposed to all that we can offer them.

My library school education was very general. I would
feel more confident with more training in "non-library"
areas such as child development and reading. And most
conference and continuing education offerings seem to
me to be repeats of the practical "how I run my
program" approach instead of bringing in experts from
other fields with new and/or theoretical programs.

I am happy that more attention is being paid to ways
librarians can serve children under three and their
parents. These are such important formative years that
I think we cannot afford to neglect the children in this
age group.

In this community, the programs are as much for social
reasons as they are for library reasons. In many one-
child families, the programs are the child's first
exposure to other children his own age. They are also
many youngster's first structured activity, where he
learns the meaning of self-control, turn-taking, accepta-
ble/unacceptable behavior, etc. In an eight-week
session, the change in a child's behavior (and attention
span!) is remarkable.

I think library service to children under three is terribly
important. Our community has responded quite favora-
bly to our weekly "Toddlertime." We have also begun a

"Toddler Collection"—a collection of sturdy board books—that has been quite popular.

Our toddler storytime is an important part of our overall programming for children. Our storytimes are planned as an introduction to our pre-school storyhours, to be a socializing experience for our young library users, and to teach them a love for books that we hope to nurture as they mature. One of the nice things that I have noticed is how friendly the children feel about each other and that the parents have gotten acquainted too. The children feel that this is their special activity. Some have older brothers and sisters who attend our older storytimes, and they enjoy a library activity planned just for them. I am pleased that the library has become such a part of their young lives.

The program has been well received by parents. I haven't used newspaper publicity since initiating the program because of the responses. Busy parents are also becoming reacquainted with the library through the program. *Everyone* is reading and looking forward to visits to the library.

In this time of the increasingly common pastime of using T.V. with children, it is more important than ever before that children learn the enjoyment of books as early as possible. There must be continuing reinforcement throughout the childhood years, always striving for the *pleasure* of reading and not a nagging "educational only" use of books. If a child learns to read well, he can master anything else he wishes to learn. If he can't read, there is little he can master.

We find that our two-year-old storytimes draw a lot of response. Children over three have other options (preschool, etc.) more readily available, but less is available for children under three. Parents and children have responded to our storytimes with enthusiasm.

Working with toddlers has been one of the most rewarding aspects of children's librarianship for me. They may not respond at the first few storytimes they attend, but after they feel comfortable in the library and sitting among peers they really show you how bright they are. Seeing them finally doing the fingerplays you've done alone for weeks (or only with their parents), and actually saying the words along with you with smiles on their faces can brighten your day. The ultimate success is having them run up to you when they come to the library—the feeling is fantastic—to know you've made them feel comfortable in *their* library and have provided the beginning of a life-long love of books. It's never too early to start!!!

My two-year-old (plus one parent) story programs have been very educational for me. I found the children shy of me *and* of each other. By the end of the twelve-week session, however, they would approach me or each other. I found them very willing to sit and listen to stories and not as willing to participate in activities, but this too changed as their shyness decreased. We use a formal, getting-ready-to-listen song at each session. Nursery rhymes (with a puppet "leader") have been most successful. A coloring page or activity sheet handout at the end of each session helped them to approach me. A display of books by authors used in story programs helps educate parents as to good types of materials for two-year-olds.

I think a lot of librarians are afraid to try programming for the young child. We haven't been doing it that long, and with the parents involved too, it is *easier* than programs for three-and-four-year-olds alone. Plus, it is a great opportunity to show parents how library materials can be used.

Our programs with toddlers are very successful. We are now looking for more programs for pre-threes. We are trying to expand our services in this direction.

We do our two-year-old programs at 6:30 p.m. This has turned out to be a good time because it gives a chance for fathers or both parents to attend.

My advice to those considering such a program is: (1) read material on the developmental stages of toddlers, (2) expose yourself to programs which already cater to this age (i.e., YWCA, day care centers, Head Start programs), (3) decide on the type of program you would be able to provide and feel comfortable delivering, and (4) take the initial plunge and give it a try! As the old adage says, "nothing ventured, nothing gained!"

Frequent inquiries about programs for two-year-olds and under led to the Tuesday Two's, a series held in alternate months for two-year-olds and their mothers. Group size is limited to 15 children and parents to allow for individual book selection and pre-program play with the library toy collection. This activity leads to a sense of familiarity with the librarian and the purpose of the program which is the child's introduction to story hour and the pleasure of books. Book talks on parenting, child development, crafts and games titles are given for parents.

We have worked very hard at establishing a preschool network—publishing a guide to area preschool services and keeping in touch with these agencies, day care centers and nursery schools.

Our library system provides a book list and general welcome-to-the-library pamphlet for new mothers. It is part of their hospital "freebies." I give a lot of attention to mothers and fathers who bring small children in, and I show them not only the picture book section, with suggestions of simple books if they want, but also where the parenting section is, and the Mother Goose collections, song books, etc. are. My goal is to encourage parents to be comfortable with their little ones in the room.

We are convinced that these programs are very beneficial to the children who attend in that they: help build language and vocabulary, a love of words and books; provide an introductory group experience; help develop self-esteem and pride in children's ability to participate

in songs, finger plays, creative dramatics, etc.; and
develop listening skills and a longer attention span.

It takes a lot of thoughtful preparation, energy, creativity, experience and a little showmanship to conduct
successful programs for this age group. The use of
visuals, props, puppets and/or physical activity is, in
my opinion, essential.

Preschool programs also provide a time for mothers to
meet each other, make new acquaintances and find
companions of the same age for their children—an
added benefit to the story programs.

I find a group of 5 to 6 works best in my weekly Toddler's
Storytime. It's marvelous to watch them develop as they
get used to the library and myself—we really have some
good times.

The need for sound, well organized, pleasurable programming for parent-child participation for toddlers is
great.

This library has had preschool story hours since about
1926, but until rather recently limited it to three- to five-
year-olds, on the theory that only above 3 can a child
happily become part of a group experience. Yet we have
given parents and caregivers advice about 'books for
babies' all along. Wish we hadn't wasted so many years
of not presenting programs for under-threes. With on-a-
parent's-lap arrangement, or just a different view of
group behavior, we do fine with babies.

The storyhour for two's and their parents is our most
popular program. We get terrific comments from those
that attend.

Librarians who are doing programs for two's and
younger really need some type of class or seminar in
early childhood development. Also reading in this area
is a must. Once a librarian has a basic understanding of
development, he/she can incorporate library activities
into an imaginative program.

Our storytimes are for two- and three-year-olds. The programs are 20 minutes long, 1 day a week for 4 weeks. I repeat the same finger plays and songs each week so that by the end of the third week the children have confidence in the program and look forward to it. Books, flannel board stories, and creative dramatics differ each week. I use only one book per session. It is asking a lot of a wiggly two-year-old to sit still and look at a storybook from a distance.

Last winter we did a Sleepy Toddler Time in the evenings for parents who worked. The toddlers were encouraged to wear their pajamas though most did not. The evening program brought in quite a few couples and fathers. Even the older children in several of the families (through pre-teen) came to watch "the baby" learn. This will definitely be a repeat program.

I enjoy this type of storyhour now; find it extremely demanding but rewarding. The parent-child pair acquire some new material and techniques for facilitating information exchange and I watch the gateways open with joy.

Some Typical Early Childhood Literature Sharing Programs

Descriptions of "typical" early childhood literature sharing programs can be drawn from a combination of the information gathered from the library literature and the information provided by the participants of the study. Even though there are probably no programs exactly like the composite ones described here, most existing programs are similar to them in the more important respects.

Several librarians, when returning their completed questionnaires, enclosed handouts designed for parents about their programs (usually storytimes) or letters explaining their particular programs. For example, I received a copy of the letter Eleanor Barksdale, Children's Librarian of the Simsbury (Connecticut) Public Library, sent to parents:

Dear Parents:

Welcome to Simsbury Public Library's Two Year Old Storytime Program. This season it will extend from (blank for filling in dates).

The format of this program is quite different than the traditional preschool storytime. Parents are asked to stay and act as role models for their children. The Librarian leads the group. The formal part of the program will last about 25 minutes, will include songs, finger plays and simple picture books. Please do not be distressed if your child does not sit and listen during the entire storytime. This is to be expected. He or she is only being a two year old. Even when he is off playing by himself he is probably listening and learning. It is hoped that his program will be an opportunity for your child to develop his or her attention span, learn group behavior as well as be introduced to books and the Library.

Please plan on arriving a few minutes early for each session so that you and your child will have a chance to feel at home.

One can see that there is quite a bit of information about the Simsbury storytime program in the above letter. From letters like this forwarded to me by various librarians and from information in the library literature, I will outline typical programs. In addition, I will pass on suggestions made by librarians to me in their correspondence.

Storytimes for Children under Three

Before beginning the program, other community agencies were contacted to see what early childhood services were already being offered. This was done to avoid duplication. The scope and goals of the program were then established. The library administration approved the storytimes program, and tie-ins with other areas of the library, such as Adult Services which provided child development materials for parents, were established.

In some libraries a parent orientation meeting planned for parents only was held in preparation for the program, usually in the early evening. Its purpose was to make the parents feel comfortable by acquainting them with the format and the purpose of the program, and demonstrating how the program would be conducted. A sample finger play was used for an example, and parents were introduced to a selection of parenting books and books appropriate for their children's age. Often handouts such as bibliographies were distributed at this meeting, which also served as a forum for parents to ask questions, and as a time for parents to meet each other in addition to the library staff.

The typical storytime was held in a room free from interruptions and distraction, or in an area of the children's room that was quiet and away from the traffic flow. The children were arranged so their backs were to any possible distractions, such as other library users walking through the room.

The children and their parents were asked to sit on the carpeted floor, carpet squares or cushions in a typical storytime semicircle with the parent directly behind the child or with the child in the adult's lap. The librarian sat on a low chair or a stool to give height so that the children could see the picture book, finger play, or flannel board story.

Nap times had to be considered when deciding on the schedule for the series. Weekday mornings around 10:00 were the most popular for children with a non-working parent or a caregiver. Early evenings around 7:00 were popular for children with working parents, but were not so well attended as the morning series.

Registration for each session was required, and was usually done by phoning the library although mail registration was also used. It was stressed that the registration should include the child's birth date. The birth date is important to be certain that the child is within the age range limits (established by the librarians in the planning stage of the series), and to determine the overall "age" of the group for the particular session so that materials and activities are appropriately geared.

The typical length of the series was from 6 to 12 weeks, with three to five series a year. The size of the group was limited by the librarian to 8 to 15 children, usually with their parents. A session lasted from 15 to 30 minutes, but the librarian had to be extremely flexible. One librarian commented that the length of the program "may be shortened or lengthened at times, depending on how restless or attentive the group is."

Parents who participated in the storytime series were asked to attend regularly and to be prompt. Since there was registration, name tags with each child's name could be prepared in advance. In some cases, name tags for parents were also prepared so that parents could get to know each other more easily. Name tags for the children were made using a heavy paper and were often cut from a simple stencil of a teddy bear, cat, dog, balloon, car, etc. A length of yarn was pulled through a reinforced hole in the name tag figure and tied in a loop large enough to fit over the child's head.

A few minutes before the storytime, children went to the librarian to get their name tags. At the conclusion of the storytime, the librarian collected the name tags to keep them for next time. At the end of the series, children kept their name tags, and many librarians commented that the children were elated to be able to take them home to show their fathers or other family members.

Parents or caregivers were informed that the librarian would appreciate feedback about reactions they noticed from their children both in the group and at home. This kind of feedback helped the librarian to evaluate the series. A record of attendance also helped in the evaluation of what time of the day was best.

At the conclusion of the series parents were asked to complete a simple questionnaire to help the librarians evaluate the program and to help in the planning of other series. The questions were usually open-ended, eliciting opinions from the parents about the activities, the length of the program, and asking participants to make suggestions for future storytimes.

Informational Programs for Parents and/or Caregivers of Young Children

The most common informational programs were for two types of audiences—organized groups, e.g., "young mothers" clubs in area churches, child care centers, etc., and individuals. Usually the library offered a program (some librarians referred to it as a workshop or a lecture) or a series of programs to individuals in the library. In the case of organized groups, the library often took the program to the group's meeting place, thereby offering an outreach service.

An example of a particular outreach informational program is one begun in 1971 by the Children's Department of the Orlando (Florida) Public Library. The "Sharing Literature with Children" program has operated on the premise that since the library was not able to reach each and every child in the community individually, the library should concentrate on teaching adults who work with children how to share literature with young children. A team of two librarians visited the group of adults, usually child care center personnel, and presented a workshop.

In the workshop, the librarian explained the rationale for bringing young children and literature together, demonstrated storytelling techniques, the use of the flannel board, finger plays, and puppetry. The presentation of materials was designed for each group, the chief characteristics being flexibility and informality.

In most cases it was the library that initiated contact for the workshop with the child care centers. One of the most effective methods of reaching the centers was to work through organized county or city agencies, using lists of licensed centers compiled by local governmental offices.

A typical informational program at the library was organized as a series of programs for parents to attend. Some of the sessions were held in the mornings and others in the evenings. Sometimes outside speakers, usually local educators, led a session instead of the librarian.

Outside speakers discussed such topics as parenting, child development and the characteristics of a young child, discipline, toilet training, and how to select and use toys. Librarians discussed such topics as library resources, how to choose books, reading aloud to your child, and how to introduce and involve the child in literature.

The sessions were scheduled to allow time for discussions between the program leader (librarian or outside speaker) and the participants. In most cases, bibliographies on the topic were handed out to the participants either before or after the session. Book displays on the topic were also prepared. In addition, if outside speakers or librarians recommended books during the session, the books were on display in multiple copies for parents to check out.

Program publicity included news releases in local papers, appearances by librarians on local television shows, spots on local radio programs, and mailings to parents' groups. (Most librarians agreed that informational programs need much more publicity than storytime programs.)

Either at the end of the session or at the conclusion of the series, participants were asked to complete a simple questionnaire to help the librarians evaluate the program and to help in the planning of future series of informational programs. Verbal feedback from participants also helped in the evaluation of the program or series.

Conclusion

The values inherent in early childhood literature sharing programs have long been recognized. Parents with the time, the serenity, and the confidence in their own literacy to do so have for generations read aloud to their own infants and small children. In many families in the past grandmothers, grandfathers, and older brothers and sisters have shared the joys of books with the family's babies.

But we are in a new age for families and for literacy and learning. Today it is more crucial than it has ever been for libraries to help provide for *all* children this seemingly simple but essential foundation for literacy and learning: being read to, sharing stories during the early years of rapid learning, long before school begins. The children of millions of illiterate and semiliterate parents are not getting this help. Thousands of young people join every day the ranks of the 27 million illiterate and 45 million marginally literate; we believe sincerely that the early childhood program described in this small book, if carried out intensively and extensively throughout the United States, could help stem the tide.

And we are not alone in believing this. The Advertising Council's Volunteer Against Illiteracy campaign which began in the media with the start of 1985 chose as the focus for its campaign a father trying valiantly but unable to read to his small child from *The Little Engine That Could.* This focus was not chosen for emotional value alone but for the fact that illiterate parents very often give as their motivation for learning to read their desire to read to their children. Only if reading is enjoyed in childhood and becomes an ingrained habit in the early years are children likely to maintain their literacy skills through high school and into the workplace. No one knows better than illiterate or semiliterate parents how important this is or senses it more truly.

More reinforcement comes from the Reality #1,
Learning Begins Before Schooling, from *Realities:
Educational Reform in A Learning Society,* the Ameri-
can Library Association's response to *A Nation at
Risk.*[2]

Research shows that children who have been exposed to
reading and other cultural experiences before they
begin school have a better chance of success in formal
learning than those who do not have this experience.
Among the most important of the preschool experiences
are the development of skills in listening, speaking, and
looking that prepare for reading and form the basis for
the enjoyment of learning. In our society, most parents
work outside the home, so all members of the family and
extended family (including grandparents and brothers
and sisters) can play important educational roles.
Family members set the stage for reading and other
learning and provide models of behavior. This family
influence in developing attitudes toward learning (often
extended by collaboration with day care, preschool, and
other community agencies) is important for the preven-
tion of deficiencies in school and beyond. Libraries
contribute to preschool learning in two ways: through
the services, programs, and materials that help parents
increase their skills and capabilities, and through
programs that serve children directly.

Library service to parents and day care staff supports
preschool learning in a variety of ways. Libraries
provide books for adults to read aloud to children.
Groups of children in child care and day care centers
and in public libraries listen to stories and act them out.
Children borrow books and records from libraries.
Toddler programs that bring very small children and
their parents to the library together provide a basis for
later, more independent use of libraries by children as
they grow older.

All these experiences for young children require action
by motivated, enthusiastic adults—adults who will
instill a love of reading. Parents, volunteers, and day
care center staff learn from librarians how to select and

use materials with children. Librarians have the skills, experience, and desire to conduct workshops for parents, older children, babysitters, early childhood specialists, teachers, and volunteers. The library has information to help parents face problems which they face daily. In some communities, multilanguage collections for parents and preschoolers are essential. Through libraries, parents can learn how to use television and newer technology, such as computers, to nurture children's creativity and confidence.

Librarians also help create community coalitions of school personnel, public librarians, members of parent-teacher groups, and others concerned with preschool learning. Public library staff who provide information and referral services help parents develop effective partnerships with schools, preschools, day care centers, and other early childhood agencies.

Unfortunately, limited funds in many of our public libraries have caused cutbacks in children's services. Day-to-day realities of operating and staffing public libraries result in the lack of a full-time children's librarian in many libraries and branches. Because of limited library staff, parents and preschool children may wait months before being able to participate in a storyhour program.

To ensure that children and their parents have library services for effective preschool learning, public officials should:
- Appropriate funds for parent education and early childhood services in public libraries, particularly those which demonstrate outreach and which promote cooperation with other educational and community agencies.

- Establish state and federal regulations for preschool day care services which mandate book and library resources as part of the basic program requirements.

With a copy of *Early Childhood Literature Sharing Programs* in hand, and the rationale—social, economic, and political—for providing such programs at hand on every side, library administrators and children's librarians are well armed to project the need and get the staff and other resources for these programs.

Appendix A

Mail Questionnaire*

**A NATIONWIDE SURVEY OF LIBRARIANS'
PRACTICES AND ATTITUDES IN SERVING
CHILDREN UNDER THREE YEARS OF AGE
AND THEIR PARENTS AND CAREGIVERS**

ANN CARLSON
INVESTIGATOR

School of Library Service
Columbia University
New York   10027

Kay Vandergrift
Dissertation Advisor

Geographic Code _____

*Original was in booklet form

This survey is designed to provide specific information about the nature of library programs for children under three years of age and for their parents/caregivers.

Each reply is coded for the geographical region from which it comes in order to validate applicability of the conclusions of the study to all kinds of public libraries in the United States.

All responses will be analyzed anonymously, and no answer will be used to identify you or your library.

There are no "right" or "wrong" answers. Please respond as honestly as you can. If you wish to comment on any questions or qualify your answers, feel free to use the space in the margins. Your comments will be read and taken into account.

Thank you for your help. It is greatly appreciated.

Please be aware that this questionnaire should be completed by someone in your library **who has conducted or is currently conducting** either or both of the following:

    -storytimes for children under three years of age,

    -informational programs or workshops for parents and/or caregivers (day care center personnel, nursery school teachers, etc.) of children under three years of age.

If you have NOT conducted either or both of these types of programs, please check the following box, stop here, and RETURN THE QUESTION-NAIRE in the envelope which is provided.

☐ I have NOT conducted library programs for children under three years of age and/or programs for their parents/caregivers.

PART I: INSTITUTIONAL PROFILE

1. Which best describes your present position?
   (circle number of answer)
       1. CHILDREN'S LIBRARIAN IN A MAIN LIBRARY
       2. CHILDREN'S LIBRARIAN IN A BRANCH LIBRARY
       3. SUPERVISOR, COORDINATOR, OR HEAD OF CHILDREN'S
          SERVICES
       4. OTHER (specify) _____

   (if supervisor, coordinator, or head) Are your responses to questions
   (such as those about budget) reflecting a system-wide or a main
   library situation? (circle number)
       1. MAIN LIBRARY ONLY
       2. SYSTEM-WIDE (specify number of branches) _____

2. Which best describes the kind of community in which your library is located?
   (circle number)
       1. RURAL
       2. SUBURBAN
       3. URBAN

3. How many full-time or full-time equivalent children's librarians are in your
   library or branch? (circle number)
       1. NO FULL-TIME CHILDREN'S LIBRARIAN
       2. ONE
       3. 2 TO 3
       4. 4 TO 5
       5. 6 OR MORE (specify number if more than 6) ___

4. What was your budget for **children's materials and programming** from LOCAL
   funding in 1981 excluding grant funding? (circle number)
       1. LESS THAN $2,000 (specify) _____
       2. $2,000 TO $4,999
       3. $5,000 TO $11,999
       4. $12,000 TO $18,999
       5. $19,000 TO $25,000
       6. MORE THAN $25,000 (specify) _____

5. Did your library receive any type of GRANT funding for either programs for
   children under three years or for program for parents/caregivers of children
   under three years of age? (circle number)
       1. NO
       2. YES
       (if yes) Indicate the **amount** of money and the **dates** for which the
   funding was provided. If more than one grant was received, please
   indicate each one.
           $_____ FROM 19 ___ TO 19 ___
           $_____ FROM 19 ___ TO 19 ___
           $_____ FROM 19 ___ TO 19 ___

6. Were outside consultants (people other than your library staff) involved in designing your programs for children under three and/or for programs for parents/caregivers of children under three years of age? (circle number)

    1. NO
    2. YES
    └▶(if yes) Please indicate the title(s) of the consultant(s). _____
_____

PART II: SERVICES PROVIDED AND PRACTICES

SECTION A: STORYTIMES

7. Does your library offer storytimes for children under three years of age which you conduct? (circle number)

    1. YES
    2. NO
    └▶(if no) Please answer the following question and then SKIP TO QUESTION 15.

    In your opinion which is the reason your library does NOT offer storytimes for children under three? (circle one number)
        1. LACK OF MONEY
        2. LACK OF KNOWING HOW TO DO STORYTIMES
        3. LACK OF SUPPORT FROM WITHIN THE LIBRARY
        4. LACK OF PUBLIC INTEREST
        5. OTHER (specify) _____
    _____

8. When did your library begin storytimes for children under three years of age? (circle number)
    1. BEFORE 1975 (specify date) _____
    2. 1975 - 1976
    3. 1977 - 1978
    4. 1979 - 1980
    5. 1981 - 1982

9. Since you offer storytimes for children under three years of age, indicate the children's age range for which your programs are designed. (write in the spaces the age ranges in months)

    _____ MONTHS TO _____ MONTHS OF AGE

10. Are your library's storytimes offered on a regularly scheduled basis (for example, an eight week period on Monday mornings)? (circle number)
    1. NO
    2. YES
    └▶(if yes) Does the same person conduct the storytimes for the duration of the series? (circle number)
        1. YES
        2. NO
        3. SOMETIMES

11. During the storytimes, do parents/caregivers stay with their children under three years of age? (circle number)
    1. NO
    2. THE CHOICE IS LEFT TO THE PARENT OR CAREGIVER
    3. YES
    ↳ (if yes) Are parents/caregivers encouraged to **actively** participate with their children in the activities presented during the storytimes? (circle number)
        1. YES
        2. NO

12. Are parents/caregivers provided with details about the books and activities (such as booklists or printed handouts of finger plays, etc.) either before or following the storytimes? (circle number)
    1. NO
    2. YES
    3. SOMETIMES

13. During storytimes, how often do you include: (circle answer after each item)

a. FINGER PLAYS	Seldom	Sometimes	Always
b. FLANNEL OR FELT BOARD STORIES	Seldom	Sometimes	Always
c. SIMPLE PUPPETS	Seldom	Sometimes	Always
d. SONGS	Seldom	Sometimes	Always
e. PUPPET SHOWS	Seldom	Sometimes	Always
f. SIMPLE POEMS	Seldom	Sometimes	Always
g. NURSERY RHYMES	Seldom	Sometimes	Always
h. CREATIVE DRAMATICS	Seldom	Sometimes	Always
i. MUSICAL ACTIVITIES	Seldom	Sometimes	Always
j. SIMPLE STORIES	Seldom	Sometimes	Always
k. MARCHING ACTIVITIES	Seldom	Sometimes	Always
l. OTHER (specify) _____	Seldom	Sometimes	Always
_____	Seldom	Sometimes	Always

14. In your storytimes, which of the following topics have your stories, poems, etc. included? (circle number or numbers)
    1. THE PARTS OF THE BODY
    2. FAMILIAR PLACES (ZOO, BEACH, ETC.)
    3. THE FAMILY
    4. PLAY
    5. PRETEND ACTIVITIES
    6. DINOSAURS
    7. COMMON ANIMALS
    8. SUPER HEROES
    9. TRAINS, CARS, PLANES
    10. NONE OF THE ABOVE

PART II: SERVICES PROVIDED AND PRACTICES

SECTION B: INFORMATIONAL PROGRAMS OR WORKSHOPS FOR PARENTS AND/OR CAREGIVERS

15. Does your library offer informational programs or workshops for parents and/or caregivers (day care center personnel, nursery school teachers, etc.) of children under three years of age which center **around literature and literature-related activities** for young children? (circle number)
    1. YES
    2. NO
    (if no) Please answer the following question and then **SKIP TO QUESTION 23.**

    In your opinion which is the reason your library does NOT offer informational programs or workshops for parents/caregivers of children under three years of age? (circle one number)
    1. LACK OF MONEY
    2. LACK OF KNOWING HOW TO DO THESE PROGRAMS
    3. LACK OF SUPPORT FROM WITHIN THE LIBRARY
    4. LACK OF PUBLIC INTEREST
    5. OTHER (specify) _____
    _____

16. For whom do you offer informational programs and workshops of children under three years of age? (circle number)
    1. ONLY FOR PARENTS
    2. ONLY FOR CAREGIVERS SUCH AS DAY CARE CENTER STAFF, ETC.
    3. FOR BOTH PARENTS AND CAREGIVERS

17. When did you **begin** informational programs or workshops for parents/caregivers of children under three years of age? (circle number)
    1. BEFORE 1975 (specify date) _____
    2. 1975-1976
    3. 1977-1978
    4. 1979-1980
    5. 1981-1982

18. Since you offer informational programs or workshops for parents and/or caregivers of children under three years of age, indicate the age range of **children** for which your programs are designed. (write in the spaces the age ranges in months)

_____ MONTHS TO _____ MONTHS OF AGE

19. During your informational programs or workshops, do you **demonstrate storytime techniques** (such as finger plays, using a flannel board, etc.) suitable for children under three years of age to parents/caregivers? (circle number)
    1. YES
    2. NO
    3. SOMETIMES

20. During your informational programs or workshops, do you show parents/caregivers a **selection of resource books** (books with finger plays, songs. poetry. bibliographies, etc.) with literature sharing ideas for children under three years of age? (circle number)
    1. YES
    2. NO
    3. SOMETIMES

21. During your informational programs or workshops, do you show parents/caregivers a **selection of books appropriate for children under three years of age**? (circle number)
    1. YES
    2. NO
    3. SOMETIMES

22. During your informational programs or workshops, which of the following do you suggest to parents/caregivers of children under three years of age? (circle number(s) of items you suggest)
    1. PLACE LARGE CLEAR PICTURES IN THE CHILD'S ENVIRONMENT
    2. SHOW CHILD PHOTOGRAPH ALBUMS WITH SNAPSHOTS OF FAMILY MEMBERS
    3. READ STORIES THAT WILL TAKE SEVERAL READING SESSIONS TO COMPLETE
    4. SIT THE CHILD ON THEIR LAPS DURING A ONE-TO-ONE STORY
    5. PROVIDE OLD GIFT CATALOGS AND COLORFUL MAGAZINES WHICH THE CHILD CAN USE
    6. VISIT THEIR PUBLIC LIBRARY ON A REGULAR BASIS
    7. PROVIDE THE CHILD WITH A VARIETY OF BOOKS INCLUDING TACTILE BOOKS (such as touch and feel books)
    8. NONE OF THE ABOVE

PART III: ATTITUDE SURVEY

SECTION A

The following statements are designed to elicit your opinion (based on your experience) about library programs for children under three years of age. Please circle the response to each statement that most closely reflects your level of agreement or disagreement, according to the following scale:

```
1. STRONGLY AGREE
2. SOMEWHAT AGREE
3. NO OPINION
4. SOMEWHAT DISAGREE
5. STRONGLY DISAGREE
```

circle the **one**
number that reflects
your attitude

* 23.   A child is ready for stories with simple plots when he/she is comfortable talking about pictures and action shown in them.   1 2 3 4 5

24.   The development of a love for books is the most important goal of library programs for children under three years of age.   1 2 3 4 5

25.   Children under three years of age have limited imaginations and do NOT enjoy "make believe" stories.   1 2 3 4 5

26.   Children under three years of age benefit from seeing a real object along with a picture of it in a story.   1 2 3 4 5

27.   After hearing a story, children under three years of age can cooperatively act it out with other children their age.   1 2 3 4 5

28.   Since parents/caregivers serve as models, children under three years of age should see them reading.   1 2 3 4 5

29.   Home-made books with various textured materials should be suggested to parents for use by their young children.   1 2 3 4 5

30.   Infants learn by using their senses: looking, listening, smelling, tasting, and touching.   1 2 3 4 5

31.   Nursery rhymes are inappropriate for children under three years of age.   1 2 3 4 5

32.   Storytimes for children under three years of age should include activities that involve the child.   1 2 3 4 5

33.   Children under three years of age are very egocentric; they believe that the world revolves around themselves.   1 2 3 4 5

34.   Children under three years of age do NOT yet fully understand the concept of sharing and are NOT yet ready for cooperative activities.   1 2 3 4 5

*not included in analysis of data

> 1. STRONGLY AGREE
> 2. SOMEWHAT AGREE
> 3. NO OPINION
> 4. SOMEWHAT DISAGREE
> 5. STRONGLY DISAGREE

circle the **one**
number that reflects
your attitude

35. It is important for young children to hear the sound of language. 1 2 3 4 5

36. Children under three years of age have the ability to listen to a simple story and create new endings to the story. 1 2 3 4 5

37. Parents or caregivers should stay with their children under three years of age during library storytimes. 1 2 3 4 5

38. The same librarian should conduct an entire series of storytimes for children under three years of age. 1 2 3 4 5

39. Parents should be encouraged to repeat storytime activities at home with their young children. 1 2 3 4 5

40. Parents and caregivers of infants should place large, clear pictures with high contrast in the infant's environment. 1 2 3 4 5

41. Children between two and three years of age are frustrated by guessing games. 1 2 3 4 5

* 42 Library programming related to children younger than 15 months of age is best designed as informational programs for parents and caregivers. 1 2 3 4 5

43. Parents and caregivers should provide magazines with which the young child can practice turning pages. 1 2 3 4 5

44. When a child nears his/her third birthday, he/she is ready for books which introduce simple concepts, such as numbers, colors, ABCs, or sizes and shapes. 1 2 3 4 5

45. Children under three years of age enjoy stories and activities that involve changes, such as day/night, weather, growing things, etc. 1 2 3 4 5

46. Children under three years of age are ready for stories that will take several reading sessions to complete. 1 2 3 4 5

47. Photograph albums with snapshots of family members are enjoyable to a child under three years of age. 1 2 3 4 5

48. Visiting the public library should be a routine that is established early in a child's life. 1 2 3 4 5

*not included in analysis of data

PART III: ATTITUDE SURVEY

SECTION B

Please circle the number of the response which most closely reflects your opinion in the following questions.

49. In your opinion which is a better indicator of appropriate stories for a young child? (circle number)
    1. THE CHILD'S **CHRONOLOGICAL** AGE
    2. THE CHILD'S **DEVELOPMENTAL** AGE

50. Which of the following reflects your opinion? (circle number)
    1. CHILDREN UNDER THREE YEARS OF AGE **DO** HAVE BOOK PREFERENCES
    2. CHILDREN UNDER THREE YEARS OF AGE **DO NOT** HAVE BOOK PREFERENCES

51. Which of the following reflects your opinion? (circle number)
    1. CHILDREN UNDER THREE YEARS OF AGE **ENJOY** REPETITION OF STORIES
    2. CHILDREN UNDER THREE YEARS OF AGE **DISLIKE** REPETITION OF STORIES

PART IV: PERSONAL PROFILE

52. How many years have you been a children's librarian? (circle number)
    1. LESS THAN 1 YEAR
    2. 1 TO 3 YEARS
    3. 4 TO 6 YEARS
    4. 7 TO 9 YEARS
    5. 10 YEARS OR MORE (specify number of years) _____

53. What is your HIGHEST level of formal education? (circle number)
    1. HIGH SCHOOL DEGREE
    2. BACHELOR'S DEGREE (specify subject) _____
    3. MASTER'S IN LIBRARY SCIENCE
    4. SUBJECT MASTER'S (specify subject) _____
    5. SUBJECT MASTER'S **PLUS** A DEGREE IN LIBRARY SCIENCE
       (specify subject) _____
    6. OTHER (specify) _____

54. Have you ever been a classroom or nursery school teacher? (circle number)
    1. NO
    ⌐ 2. YES
    ↳(if yes) Indicate the age of children taught. _____

55. Are you a parent? (circle number)
    1. NO
    2. YES

56. Which describe(s) your training for working with children under three years of age? (circle number or numbers)
    1. ON-THE-JOB TRAINING
    2. PERSONAL READING IN EARLY CHILDHOOD DEVELOPMENT
    3. FORMAL COURSES IN EARLY CHILDHOOD EDUCATION
    4. SPECIALIZATION OR DEGREE IN EARLY CHILDHOOD EDUCATION
    5. NONE OF THE ABOVE

57. Approximately how many books or articles concerning early childhood development did you read during the past year? (circle number)
    1. NONE
    2. 1 TO 10
    3. 11 TO 25
    4. MORE THAN 25

58. Do you belong to any professional organizations ? (circle number)
    1. NO
    ⌐ 2. YES
    ↳ (if yes) Indicate which ones. (circle the number(s) of all those that apply)
        1. AMERICAN LIBRARY ASSOCIATION (ALA)
        2. ASSOCIATION FOR LIBRARY SERVICE TO CHILDREN (ALSC)
        3. OTHER DIVISIONS OR COMMITTEES OF ALA (specify) _____
        _____
        4. YOUR STATE LIBRARY ASSOCIATION
        5. ANY EARLY CHILDHOOD EDUCATION ORGANIZATIONS (specify) _____
        6. OTHER RELEVANT ORGANIZATIONS _____
        _____
        _____

If you wish to make any comments, feel free to use this space.

Thank you for your cooperation.

Appendix B

Additional Tables Relating to Analysis of the Data

Table 1
Anova Table: Index of Attitudes X if Grant Funding for Programs Was Received

Dependent variable: INDEX OF ATTITUDES
Independent variable: IF GRANT FUNDING WAS
RECEIVED

ONEWAY ANOVA:	sums of squares	degrees of freedom	mean square
Between groups	.2370	1	.2370
Within groups	12.1955	231	.0528
Total	12.4325	232	—

Librarian Received Grant Funding	Mean	Number
Yes	1.618	37
No	1.705	196
Total	1.692	233
F = 4.4888	p-value = .0352	

Table 2
Anova Table: Index of Attitudes X if Librarian Has Past Teaching Experience

Dependent variable: INDEX OF ATTITUDES
Independent variable: IF LIBRARIAN HAS PAST
TEACHING EXPERIENCE

ONEWAY ANOVA:	sums of squares	degrees of freedom	mean square
Between groups	.2987	1	.2987
Within groups	12.1329	230	.0528
Total	12.4316	231	—

Librarian Has Past Teaching Experience	Mean	Number
Yes	1.648	93
No	1.721	139
Total	1.692	232

F = 5.6622	p-value = .0182

Table 3
Anova Table: Index of Attitudes
X if Librarian Has Taken Early
Childhood Education Courses

Dependent variable: INDEX OF ATTITUDES
Independent variable: IF LIBRARIAN HAS TAKEN
EARLY CHILDHOOD EDUCA-
TION COURSES

ONEWAY ANOVA:	sums of squares	degrees of freedom	mean square
Between groups	.4000	1	.4000
Within groups	12.0316	230	.0523
Total	12.4316	231	—

Librarian Has Taken Early Childhood Education Courses	Mean	Number
Yes	1.643	98
No	1.727	134
Total	1.692	232
F = 7.6461	p-value = .0062	

Table 4
Anova Table: Index of Attitudes X Librarian's Amount of Early Childhood Development Reading

Dependent variable: INDEX OF ATTITUDES
Independent variable: LIBRARIAN'S AMOUNT OF
EARLY CHILDHOOD DEVELOP-
MENT READING

ONEWAY ANOVA:	sums of squares	degrees of freedom	mean square
Between groups	.7262	3	.2421
Within groups	11.7054	228	.0513
Total	12.4316	231	—

Number of Books or Articles Read	Mean	Number
None	1.963	4
1 - 10	1.720	130
11 - 25	1.658	80
More than 25	1.577	18
Total	1.692	232

F = 4.7148   p-value = .0033

Table 5
Anova Table: Index of Attitudes X if Librarian Offers Informational Programs

Dependent variable: INDEX OF ATTITUDES
Independent variable: IF LIBRARIAN OFFERS
INFORMATIONAL PROGRAMS

ONEWAY ANOVA:	sums of squares	degrees of freedom	mean square
Between groups	.8920	1	.8920
Within groups	11.5405	231	.0500
Total	12.4325	232	—

Librarian Offers Informational Programs	Mean	Number
Yes	1.629	115
No	1.752	118
Total	1.692	233

F = 17.8536	p-value = .0001

Table 6
Contingency Table:
If Grant Funding for Programs Was Received X Librarian's Amount of Early Childhood Development Reading

Number of Books or Articles Read	Grant Funding Received		
	Yes	No	Total
None	0 (0%)*	4 (2%)	4
1 - 10	15 (38.5%)	122 (57%)	137
11 - 25	19 (48.7%)	72 (34%)	91
More than 25	5 (12.8%)	15 (7%)	20
Total	39	213	252

*(column percentage)

Table 7
Contingency Table:
If Early Childhood Education Courses Were Taken X Librarian's Amount of Early Childhood Development Reading

Number of Books or Articles Read	Taken Courses		
	Yes	No	Total
None	1 (.9%)*	3 (2.1%)	4
1 - 10	48 (44.9%)	89 (61.4%)	137
11 - 25	49 (45.8%)	42 (29%)	91
More than 25	9 (8.4%)	11 (7.6%)	20
Total	107	145	252

*(column percentage)

Table 8
Contingency Table:
If Librarian Has Past Teaching
Experience X Librarian's Amount of
Early Childhood Development Reading

Number of Books or Articles Read	Past Teaching Experience		Total
	Yes	No	
None	1 (1%)*	3 (2%)	4
1 - 10	50 (48.5%)	87 (58.4%)	137
11 - 25	39 (37.9%)	52 (34.9%)	91
More than 25	13 (12.6%)	7 (4.7%)	20
Total	103	149	252

*(column percentage)

Notes

1. Development of Library Programs for Children under Three Years of Age and for Parents and Caregivers

1. Clarence W. Sumner, *The Birthright of Babyhood* (New York: Thomas Nelson and Sons, 1936), 43, ix.

2. ALA Committee on Cooperation with the National Congress of Parents and Teachers, *The Parents' Bookshelf* (Chicago: American Library Association, 1929).

3. L.A. Palmer, *Play Life in the First Eight Years* (Boston: Ginn, 1916); Charlotte Garrison, *Permanent Play Materials for Young Children* (New York: Scribner, 1926); J.C. Fenton, *A Practical Psychology of Babyhood* (Boston: Houghton, 1925); W.P. Lucas, *Health of the Run-about Child* (New York: Macmillan, 1924); R.M. Smith, *From Infancy to Childhood* (Boston: Atlantic Monthly, 1925).

4. William Bristow, "The Adult Education Program of the National Congress of Parents and Teachers," in *The Role of the Library in Adult Education*, Louis R. Wilson, ed. (Chicago: University of Chicago Press, 1937), 87-103.

5. *Library Literature* 1936-1939 (New York: H.W. Wilson, 1940), 1014.

6. John W. Creager, "Parents Find New Users for the Library," *Wilson Bulletin for Librarians* 11 (September 1936):35-37.

7. Clarence W. Sumner, *The Birthright of Babyhood* (New York: Thomas Nelson and Sons, 1936), 41-42.

8. Martha M. Goodman, "First Mothers' Institute," *Library Journal* 61 (15 April 1936):314-15.

9. Garry C. Myers and Clarence W. Sumner, *Books and Babies* (Chicago: McClurg, 1938), 38.

10. Goodman, "First Mothers' Institute," 314.

11. "New Angle of Service," *Library Journal* 63 (1 March 1938):171.

12. Goodman, "First Mothers' Institute," 315.

13. Myers and Sumner, *Books and Babies,* 25.

14. Myers and Sumner, *Books and Babies,* 9.

15. Sumner, *The Birthright of Babyhood,* viii.

16. Ruth Budd Galbraith, "Storytelling: A Wartime Activity," *Wilson Library Bulletin* 17 (May 1943):723.

17. One article, in particular, provides a summary of parent education programs from 1937 to 1946. Elizabeth M. Smith, "The Public Library Contributes to Parent Education," *Library Journal* (15 October 1946):1427-32.

18. For example: Vardine Moore, *Pre-School Story Hour,* 2nd ed. (Metuchen, N.J.: Scarecrow Press, 1972), and Ellin Greene, "The Preschool Story Hour Today," *Top of the News* 31 (November 1974):80-85.

19. "Just under Three Is a Little too Young," *Library Journal* 76 (15 April 1951):694-95.

20. Ethel C. Karrick, "The Preschool Story Hour," *ALA Bulletin* 41 (November 1947):447.

21. Ethel Heins and Ferne Johnson, "Start Early for an Early Start," *Top of the News* 31 (November 1974):39.

22. Sandra Sivulich, "Idea Exchange: Public Libraries and Early Childhood Education," *PLA Newsletter* 16 (Spring 1977):4-6; Diana Young, "Parents, Children, Libraries," *PLA Newsletter* 16 (Winter 1977):16, Faith Hektoen, "Parent Support Programs," *PLA Newsletter* 16 (Winter 1977):16-17; Ferne Johnson, ed., *Start Early for an Early Start* (Chicago: ALA, 1976); Orlando Public Library, *What's so Great about Books?* (16mm, 15 min., color, 1977).

23. Linda Blaha, "An Information and Referral Service for Parents of Preschool Children," *Top of the News* 33 (Summer 1977):360-63.

24. Carolyn S. Peterson, "Sharing Literature with Children," in *Start Early for an Early Start,* Ferne Johnson, ed. (Chicago: ALA, 1976), pp. 100-104; Jean Rustici, "Public Library and Child Care Center Relationship," *PLA Newsletter* 16 (Winter 1977):17-18; Penny Wilson and Peggy Abramo, "Early Childhood Programs for Adults—Public Library Reaches Out," *Connecticut Libraries* 15 (June 1973):10-11.

25. Faith Hektoen, "Parent Support Programs," *PLA Newsletter* 16 (Winter 1977):16-17; Martha Barnes, "Library Service to Very Young Children and Their Parents in Westchester County," *Bookmark* 37 (Summer 1978):116-18; Nancy DeSalvo, "The Terrific Two's: Pilot Program for Parents and Two Year Olds," *Connecticut Libraries* 19 (April 1977):13-17.

26. Grace Ruth, "Parenting Collection," in *Start Early for an Early Start,* Ferne Johnson, ed. (Chicago: ALA, 1976), pp. 151-154.

27. S.S. Cherry, "Preschool Programs Stimulate Tots, Educate Adults," *American Libraries* 25 (April 1979):204.

28. "Toys for Loan: A New Library Service," *Library Journal* 99 (15 April 1974):1176; Nancy Young Orr, "Toys that Teach," in *Start Early for an Early Start,* Ferne Johnson, ed. (Chicago: ALA, 1976), pp. 22-28.

29. "Revamped Ohio Library Opens 'Discovery Center,'" *School Library Journal* 25 (September 1978):13; and, "Model Preschool Center Set up by Ohio Library," *Library Journal* 103 (15 March 1978):606, "S.C. Library to Pioneer Service to Toddlers," *Library Journal* 103 (15 April 1977):868; "Project Little Kids Lauded by HEW," *Library Journal* 104 (15 February 1979):450.

30. Juliet K. Markowsky, "Storytime for Toddlers," *School Library Journal* 23 (May 1977):28-31; DeSalvo, "The Terrific Two's: Pilot Program for Parents and Two Year Olds," 13-17; Barnes, "Library Service to Very Young Children and Their Parents in Westchester County," 116-18; Nancy Kewish, "South Euclid's Pilot Project for Two-Year-Olds and Parents," *School Library Journal* 25 (March 1979):93-98; Bonnie S. Fowler, "Toddlers' Storytimes," *North Carolina Libraries* 38 (Summer 1981):21-24.

31. Seven Parent Projects Awarded CBC Grants," *School Library Journal* 25 (September 1978):14; Helen Cannon and Joyce Dixon, "Parents, New Babies, and Books," *School Library Journal* 24 (January 1978):68.

32. Amy Kellman, "Service to Preschoolers and Adults," in *Children's Services of Public Libraries,* Selma Richardson, ed. (Urbana-Champaign: University of Illinois, Graduate School of Library Science, 1978), 99.

2. Overviews of Recent Changes in the Study of Early Childhood Development

1. Carl Murchison and Suzanne Langer, trans., "Tiedemann's Observations on the Development of the Mental Faculties of Children," *Pedagogical Seminary and Journal of Genetic Psychology* 34 (1927):205-30.

2. Carl Murchison and Suzanne Langer, trans., "Tiedemann's Observations on the Development of the Mental Faculties of Children," 205.

3. Jerome Kagan, *The Growth of the Child: Reflections on Human Development* (New York: Norton, 1978), 21.

4. See J.H. Flavell, *The Developmental Psychology of Jean Piaget* (Princeton: Van Nostrand, 1963) for information about research during the 1930s to 1960s; however, not until the 1960s did psychologists in the U.S. begin to seriously consider Piaget's theories.

5. Paul Mussen, *The Psychological Development of the Child*, 2d ed. (Englewood Cliffs, N.J.: Prentice-Hall, 1973), xi.

6. Leonard Carmichael, ed., *Manual of Child Psychology* (New York: John Wiley & Sons, 1946), and *Manual of Child Psychology,* 2d ed. (New York: John Wiley & Sons, 1954); Paul Mussen, ed., *Carmichael's Manual of Child Psychology*, 3d ed. (New York: John Wiley & Sons, 1970).

7. Karl Pratt, "The Neonate," in *Manual of Child Pscyhology,* Leonard Carmichael, ed. (1946), 190-255; and 2d ed. (1954), 215-91; William Kessen, Marshall Haith and Philip Salapatek, "Human Infancy," in *Carmichael's Manual of Child Psychology,* Paul Mussen, ed., 3d ed. (1970), 287-446.

8. Kurt Lewin, "Behavior and Development as a Function of the Total Situation," in *Manual of Child Psychology* (1946), 791-844, and 2d ed. (1954), 918-70.

9. Burton White, *The First Three Years of Life* (Englewood Cliffs, N.J.: Prentice-Hall, 1975), xi.

10. Benjamin Bloom, *Stability and Change in Human Character* (New York: John Wiley & Sons, 1964).

11. Arnold Gesell, Frances Ilg, and Louise Ames, *Infant and Child in the Culture of Today,* rev. ed. (New York: Harper & Row, 1974); T. Berry Brazelton, *Infants and Mothers* (New York: Delacorte Press, 1969), and *Toddlers and Parents* (New York: Delacorte Press, 1975); Ira Gordon, *Baby Learning through Baby Play* (New York: St. Martin's Press, 1970), and *Baby to Parent, Parent to Baby* (New York: St. Martin's Press, 1977); Ira Gordon, B. Guinagh and R. Jester, *Child Learning through Child Play* (New York: St. Martin's Press, 1972).

12. A full account of Project Head Start is located in: Westinghouse Learning Corporation, "The Impact of Head Start," in *Revisiting Early Childhood Education,* Joe Frost, ed. (New York: Holt, Rinehart & Winston, 1973).

13. A comprehensive review is located in: Alice S. Honig, *Parent Involvement in Early Childhood Education,* rev. ed. (Washington, D.C.: National Association for the Education of Young Children, 1979).

14. Urie Bronfenbrenner, *Is Early Intervention Effective?: A Report on Longitudinal Evaluation of Preschool Programs,* vol. II (Washington, D.C.: Office of Child Development, U.S. Dept. of HEW, 1974), 55.

3. Developing the Rationale for Introducing Young Children to Literature

1. Dorothy Butler, *Babies Need Books* (New York: Atheneum, 1980), viii.

2. Linda Lamme, *Raising Readers: A Guide to Sharing Literature with Young Children* (New York: Walker, 1980), xiii.

3. Aidan Chambers, *Introducing Books to Children* (London: Heinemann, 1973), 3.

4. Dorothy Butler, *Babies Need Books;* Susan M. Glazer, *Getting Ready to Read: Creating Readers from Birth through Six* (Englewood Cliffs, N.J.: Prentice-Hall, 1980); Linda Lamme, *Raising Readers: A Guide to Sharing Literature with Young Children.*

5. Annis Duff, *"Bequest of Wings": A Family's Pleasure with Books* (New York: Viking, 1944); May Lamberton Becker, *First Adventures in Reading: Introducing Children to Books* (New York: F.A. Stokes, 1936); Dorothy White, *Books before Five* (New York: Oxford University Press, 1954); Nancy Larrick, *A Parent's Guide to Children's Reading* (New York: Doubleday, 1958).

6. Linda Lamme, "Library Programs for Infants and Toddlers: An Educator's View," adapted from a speech given at the Florida Library Association Annual Meeting, Orlando, Florida, 13 May, 1979 (Tallahassee, Fla.: Florida State Library, 1979), 2-4, 7-8.

7. J.H. Flavell, *Cognitive Development* (Englewood Cliffs, N.J.: Prentice-Hall, 1977), 62.

8. William H. Teal, "Positive Environments for Learning to Read: What Studies of Early Readers Tell Us," *Language Arts* 55 (November/December 1978):922-32.

9. L.J. Stone and J. Church, *Childhood and Adolescence,* 4th ed. (New York: Random House, 1979).

10. E.W. Willemsen, *Understanding Infancy* (San Francisco: W.H. Freeman & Company, 1979).

11. J. Piaget and B. Inhelder, *The Psychology of the Child* (New York: Basic Books, 1969); J. Piaget, *Construction of Reality in the Child* (New York: Basic Books, 1954); J. Piaget, *The Origins of*

Intelligence in the Child (New York: Norton, 1963); J. Piaget, *Play, Dreams and Imitation in Childhood* (New York: Norton, 1962).

12. Erik Erikson, *Childhood and Society,* 2d rev. ed. (New York: Norton, 1963).

13. R.R. Sears, E. Maccoby and H. Levin, *Patterns of Child Rearing* (New York: Harper & Row, 1957); R.R. Sears, *Identification and Child Rearing* (Stanford, Cal.: Stanford University Press, 1965); and R.R. Sears and S.S. Feldman, *The Seven Ages of Man* (New York: Kaufman, 1973).

14. J. McV. Hunt, *Intelligence and Experience* (New York: Ronald Press, 1961); I.C. Uzgiris and J. McV. Hunt, *Assessment in Infancy* (Urbana: University of Illinois Press, 1975); I.C. Uzgiris, "Organization of Sensorimotor Intelligence," in *Origins of Intelligence*, M. Lewis, ed. (New York: Wiley, 1976).

15. T.G.R. Bower, *A Primer of Infant Development* (San Francisco: W.H. Freeman & Co., 1977); T.G.R. Bower, *Development in Infancy* (San Francisco: W.H. Freeman & Co., 1974).

16. P. Dale, *Language Development* (New York: Holt, Rinehart & Winston, 1976).

17. A. Gesell, F. Ilg and L. Ames, *Infant and Child in the Culture of Today,* rev. ed. (New York: Harper & Row, 1974); L. Ames, et al., *The Gesell Institute's Child from One to Six* (New York: Harper & Row, 1979).

18. B.L. White, *Human Infants: Experience and Psychological Development* (Englewood Cliffs, N.J.: Prentice-Hall, 1971); B.L. White and J.C. Watts, *Experience and Environment* (Englewood Cliffs, N.J.: Prentice-Hall, 1973).

19. B.L. White, *The First Three Years of Life* (Englewood Cliffs, N.J.: Prentice-Hall, 1975); M.A.S. Pulaski, *Your Baby's Mind and How It Grows: Piaget's Theory for Parents* (New York: Harper & Row, 1978); C. Tomlinson-Keasey, *Child's Eye View* (New York: St. Martin's Press, 1980).

20. B.M. Caldwell, "A Day at the Kramer Baby House," in *Developing Programs for Infants and Toddlers,* Monroe D. Cohen, ed. (Washington, D.C.: Association for Childhood Educational International, 1977), 34-51.

21. B.L. White, *The First Three Years of Life,* 232.

22. D.N. Stern, *The First Relationship: Mother and Infant* (Cambridge, Mass.: Harvard University Press, 1977).

23. The SCSS Conversational System was used. Norman H. Nie et al., *SCSS: A User's Guide to the SCSS Conversational System* (New York: McGraw-Hill, 1980).

4. The Schema

1. Recognition memory exists before this time, usually at approximately three months of age.

2. Curiosity is present from birth but it becomes more noticeable when the child becomes mobile.

3. One of the limitations of interpreting the characteristics of social development is a culturally-bound subjectivity.

6. Analysis of the Data

1. The questionnaire contained 26 statements. However, data from two statements were not analyzed since comments from participants suggested that these were ambiguous statements. See Appendix A for statements not included in the analysis of data.

7. The Programs: Details and Comments

1. I consulted with over a dozen colleagues who were nursery school teachers of two-year-olds, as I was, about the topics of dinosaurs and superheroes. All agreed that these two topics were of interest to groups of children over three years of age.

2. American Library Association. *Realities: Educational Reform in A Learning Society.* (Chicago: American Library Association, 1984.)

Index